I0221585

Orville Ward Owen

The Historical Tragedy of Mary Queen of Scots

Orville Ward Owen

The Historical Tragedy of Mary Queen of Scots

ISBN/EAN: 9783337324513

Printed in Europe, USA, Canada, Australia, Japan

Cover: Foto ©ninafisch / pixelio.de

More available books at **www.hansebooks.com**

THE

HISTORICAL TRAGEDY

OF

MARY QUEEN OF SCOTS.

BY THE AUTHOR OF

HAMLET, RICHARD III,. OTHELLO,
AS YOU LIKE IT, ETC.

DECIPHERED

FROM THE WORKS OF

SIR FRANCIS BACON

BY

ORVILLE W. OWEN, M. D.

DETROIT, MICH. :
HOWARD PUBLISHING COMPANY.

LONDON :
GAY & BIRD, 5, CHANDOS STREET.

Copyright, 1894.
By ORVILLE W. OWEN.
All rights reserved.

PUBLISHER'S NOTE.

This Tragedy is produced by the application of the Cipher rule or system, discovered by Doctor Orville W. Owen, of Detroit, in the Shakespeare plays and other works of Francis Bacon. No word of it is taken from any other source, and it is put together according to the methods described in the previous books of the Cipher series issued by this Company.

Those unfamiliar with the Cipher discoveries may be assisted in their appreciation of the Tragedy, by knowing that in the former publications it is revealed that Bacon was the son of Elizabeth, and that his father was Robert Dudley, Earl of Leicester.

This Tragedy forms part of the fourth book of Bacon's Cipher Story. A fifth and a sixth book are in preparation. Persons who may doubt that this Tragedy is the work of Francis Bacon, or that it and the previously published Cipher writings are derived through the Cipher system in the manner set forth by Doctor Owen, are invited to consider the question: *If Bacon did not write these Cipher works, who did?*

HOWARD PUBLISHING COMPANY.

Detroit, Mich., December, 1894.

The Tragedy of Mary Queen of Scots.

Actus Primus.   Scena Prima.

(Audience Room of the Palace).
Enter QUEEN ELIZABETH, *reading a letter, and*
MASTER FRANCIS BACON.

Queen Elizabeth. Master Bacon, if it is true that the Scottish Queen hath said and written thus, what particular and convenient laws have we to tame this wanton?

Francis Bacon. Madam, if it be believed that her grace doth allege this, it is merely sophistry. Still, for your honor and your safety, I would surely prove upon her person, these heinous and many manifest treasons. I grieve to hear of her seeming murderous deeds,

"But if the lamb should let the lion way,
By my advice, the lamb should lose her life."

Q. E. She shall give me but way.

F. B. But yet I would be fully satisfied she spake thus.

Q. E. My lady for this tale, is bespoke by the deathsman.[1]

F. B. I'm sorry for't; but as a counsellor, I may not in any way sustain her. You are our only rightful sovereign, and according to the laws of England, the minute whosoever speaks in tropical and abused sense, about the succession, is in the statute law upon evidence, please your Highness, a traitor: and if any subject, or person in England, send in secret, letters unto an opposed King; or instruct, consent, or seek to make away, remove, place in peril, or murder their true sovereign Queen; or touch to her prejudice her good person; or pry into the

---

1. "Said the queen, (I remember it for the efficacy of the phrase,)

[Note discourse between Bacon and the Decipherer at end of first act. In deciphering, the explanatory words of Bacon, found in the numbered foot notes, occur at points in the play, indicated by like numerals.]

princes' title, they are guilty of treason, and are rebels
recreants and traitors. And if they advise, or suffer to be
made, approaches upon England, either by invasion or
interruption of traffic; or enter into league with foreign
princes without the sovereign's will or state's allowance,
they shall be apprehended as traitors and rebels, and answer to the attainder. And in this dangerous suspect,
dread sovereign, this gilded serpent in mine opinion
lies. Nay, more; if that her Majesty while within this
kingdom, hath stirred up or made suit unto the King of
France, and doth challenge your Majesty's right to be,
by the grace of God, Queen of England, France and
Ireland, she is a silly woman, and doth show a weak
mind: for she, by my troth, is placed in the double and
odious position of a neutral, charged with treachery and
rebellion; and it is the law that such a person is a traitor,
and may suffer death by hanging or the sword, according to the will of the court.

Q. E. Yea, is it so? I will myself speak with this
woman.

F. B. Save your grace! What means your grace?
To have conference with your cousin alone?

Q. E. Aye, I do so. I will, by visiting this sweet
Queen—this subtle-witted, life-rendering politician—find
out her attributes. 'Shrew my heart! ere I taste bread,
I will unto this planetary plague.
Is she as tall as me?

F. B. She is not, madam.

Q. E. Didst hear her speak?
Is she shrill tongued or low?

F. B. Madam, I heard her speak; she is low-voiced.

Q. E. That's not so good.

What majesty is in her gait, remember
If e'er thou look'dst on majesty?

F. B. Dread madam, she hath an inferior form to you.

Q. E. Let not thy lips skip one word.

F. B. Then I say, look not upon her but when you
are well pleased.

Q. E. Hold your peace! if this prove true, she shall
pay for't. By mine honor, I would see her though I knew
I would be damned for't. Go have my Lord Leicester
here: I would speak with him. [2]

(*Enter Leicester.*)

My lord, all hail! we would visit the virtuous lady, Queen
of Scotland, at the poor castle where she lies, that she may
boast she hath beheld the English Queen.

Lord Leicester. Good madam, have you eaten on the
insane root that takes the reason prisoner?

Q. E. What, my lord! Must we fear this red-tailed
bumble-bee, and fall down and knee the way unto her
mercy, and in humbleness speak her praise and glory?
Excellent! She, of all alive, is most worthy to be praised,
being derived by descent from Henry Seventh, and that
doth call us the issue of our mother's womb, but none of
our father's kind, and not of his begetting. Didst thou note
the last shameful speech of this modest lady? That we
are a bastard, and raisèd out of the dust to be sovereign
of England? These twenty years have we suffered by her
arts—we fear her not. But, my lord, speak the truth
truly. Hast thou never found the way to the forefended
place?

L. L. No, by mine honor, madam, I never could
endure her?

_____

2. "Said she, when I had brought him to her,—

Q. E. Then be not familiar with her.

L. L. Madam, I looked on her, but I noted her not.

Q. E. Thou tellest us to keep at home. Suppose, sir, we should have thee wedded unto this mortal Venus, this heart-blood of beauty, this love's invisible soul?

L. L. Who, thy cousin Helen?

Q. E. No sir, Cressida; thou art not Paris, thou art Troilus. How likest thou our choice?

L. L. Sweet Queen, you are pleasant with me, but, dear Queen, be not my lord Pandarus.

Q. E. Sweet Queen, sweet Queen! that's a sweet Queen, i' faith, and to make a sweet lady sad, is a sour offence, but that shall not serve thy turn, that shall it not, la. We care not for such words. No, no, my lord, make no excuse, my dear honey-sweet lord, thou shalt not bob us out of our melody with broken music. We'll hear thee sing—wilt thou have us go without thee, my lord?

L. L. No, no! No such matter, you are wide.

Q. E. Yet thou makest excuse, my lord; is the fair forlorn Queen of Scotland sole possessor of thy love? Is this the cause that thou fail us? Thou art undutiful and perjured; by Holy Paul, we tell ye, we will (be assured) confer with her, in spite of thee or any of thy faction. A plague upon ye all that hath not honesty or grace!

L. L. Your grace speaks against your meetest vantage; you mistake the matter; the tender love I bear your grace, makes me most forward in this princely presence. I fear for you; should the discontented men who owe allegiance to the Scottish Queen, take note of your bold trust, they will by interception, strike at your life. [3]

---

3. " The queen started, a little and said :—

Q. E. By my faith, my lord, I thank you; yet I will go maugre Scotland's might. Hie away as swift as swallow flies, and furnish me conveyance. Come! away! away! I will go even now! in God's name away! and lose no time.

L. L. Fair Queen, your fair cousin is not here in London.

Q. E. How! Not in London? I see you make sport of me.

L. L. May it please your Highness to hear me speak?

Q. E. Yes, sir, yes.

L. L. Your Majesty would not suffer your cousin to come.

Q. E. Well said, my lord; I do remember; but can you not bring her hither, where I may have chance to speak to her?

L. L. Aye, I promise you; I'll send for her to my house; and then if your Highness vouchsafe to sup with me, you may without public proceedings, (if your royal grace wish) come to speech of her.

Q. E. Pray ye, my lord, go. [4]

L. L. Here, Talbot;   (*Enter Talbot.*)
Go you to Queen Mary and most affectionately say, I, to make atonement between us, humbly beseech her grace to come in secret to my house. And be sure you be not robbed of this lovely lady; have soldiers to attend you on horseback; ride post, and fetch her to my house; hem her train in that not a man or woman escape. Away!

. *Talbot.* My lord, I'll go tonight.

L. L. Good! I have trust and faith in you.
Fare you well!   (*Exit Talbot.*)

---

4. " My father, losing no time, calleth one of his valiant gentlemen and saith to him :—

Scena Secunda. [5]

(*Banquet Room in* LEICESTER'S *House.*)
MARY QUEEN OF SCOTS *and the* EARL OF LEICESTER *at table.*
Enter QUEEN ELIZABETH *in disguise; hides behind statue.*

Queen Mary. Better were it this woman Elizabeth
   died ;
And, noble lord, I prithee join with me
In my attempts, and I, in marriage will
Confer myself on you, if you, my lord,
Will accept me.   I am young, and apt, and fair
As is the youngest maid ; and of descent
As good as this old fox : be pitiful
Dear lord, and grant my suit.   The child that shall descend
From the true fountain of our marriage,
Will then be heir unto the lines of France,
Scotland and England.

   L. L. But your own son doth wear the crown of
      Scotland.

   Q. M. What though he do?   By act of Parliament,

---

5. "The servant bringeth the poor soul (with a small
number of friends) to my father's house, where my father doth
greet her and bid her into supper; then he sends to the Queen
and she hies her in all post there, and, like a cunning and pro-
fessed tyrant, she (after her custom) comes soft into my father's
house, and maskt by one of the statues placed in the room,
hears my lord dissemble with her grace.   This banquet did
prove as ominous to Mary, as Progene's to the adulterous
Thracian king, that fed upon the substance of his child ; for his
foxship led her into blindness with base thoughts.   The savour
of the celestial food of love, on which my lord fed her, caused
her to beg relief of him.   Said she:—

We will blot him out.   Sir, when the Scottish lords,
Did break their oaths to me, and drave me hence,
(For by their consent, and for his sake,
I was made to yield the crown and fly,)
My love did turn to hate: therefore, my lord,
'Tis but reason that I yield you my hand:
You shall have all.

    L. L. But if your title to the crown be weak,
As may appear by your son's good success,
Then were I loath to link myself with you.
James now doth live in Scotland at his ease,
And the houses of York and Lancaster
Uphold the arm of Queen Elizabeth;
On neither law nor right rests your estate;
You are an exile, and so must you stay
Until your son is brought within your power.
By this alliance what shall I win?

    Q. M. Aye, good my lord, they have through
        treachery,
Bestow'd the kingdom on my abortive son.
But I tell thee, I will requite it on them;
If that thy friends will pawn their swords for me
And my enfranchisement, demand thy fill.
If thou wilt marry me, as man and wife
Being two, are one in love, so we'll combine
In one the French, English and Scottish realms:
I swear to thee, that thou shalt be the king
Of these kingdoms; then unsheathe thy sword,
And give just sentence on this bastard Queen,
Who in the regal throne of England sits,
Which, in God's name, my lord, we will ascend.
Choose thou for thy bride, a loving handmaid

For thy desires, and not the old bastard daughter
Of that harlot-strumpet, Anne Bullen.
What sayeth my sweet lord? [6]

(ELIZABETH, *with a cry comes forth.*)

Q. E. Doth Scotland make your Majesty our judge?

Q. M. Alas! I am undone; it is the Queen!

Q. E. Nay, answer us what thou hast said of us. [7]

Why! how new, Queen? What is the matter now?
By th' rood, thou didst speak vilely of us, even now,
But we'll proclaim thee, out of hand, our sovereign,
And thou shalt reign; and thy son and heirs may claim
      our realm.
Thou hast disinherited thine only son
But thou shalt yet have children by my lord;
To him we'll yield obedience, as to a king:
Why should we not? Pray, pardon us sweet Earl;
Thy grace, like good Pierce of Exton,
(Who with the king's blood stain'd the king's own land,)
Can rid this fair and spotless innocence
Of her foul foe.
Thou scarlet sin; when thou didst speak so rash,
Thou knewest not that we were within hearing;
Thou hast undone thy life!
Thy dearest heart-blood we will have, foul wretch!
By heaven! when thou in hateful practice spak'st against
Our mother's honor, know'st thou not thou gav'st
The warrant to the executioner for thy head?
Thou, that rob'st me of my lord—

---

6. "At this, Elizabeth did cry out, and straightway came forth and said:—

7. "When death's approach is seen, 'twill not look so terrible as did Elizabeth.

Q. M. Madam, 'tis you that rob me of my lord.

Q. E. Be still! Speak not! On capital treason,
We will arrest thee and, in thy arrest,
Foul traitor, thou wilt come to know our mind.

Q. M. May't please your highness to resolve me now?

Q. E. Aye then, madam, since thou enforceth us,
We will satisfy thee: thy neck must stoop.
We'll have thy head and set it on our gates,
So thou may'st overlook the town. [8]

Q. M. How! what? no, no, noble madam, you speak
In sport I know; Your grace's words, forsooth,
Are stern, but yet no outward actions show
That you intend to wed me unto Death.
This is the English, not the Turkish court:
You'll let me live—I am too young to die!
You speak in merriment to frighten me!
Do you not speak in jest?

Q. E. Thou wretch! With idle tongue thou questionest.

Speak we no English but gibberish, or rather such,
As in old time, Evander's mother spake?
Had we not seen thee and heard thee speak,
With show of virtue daub'd with vice,
These very words that did infer our bastardy,
We could, i'th' Lethe of our angry soul,
Drown the remembrance of those wrongs, which thou
Hast done to us; but that our ears should hear thee
Telling my lord the reasons why our father,
Who now hath done his shift, did slay our mother—
By God's Mother, thou shalt post to heaven!
Think'st thou we jest now?

---

8. " The poor innocent thus began :—

And leave, nor name, nor issue, on the earth of thee;
We will take order that thy son shall fall;
The plough shall furrow where thy palace stood,
And fury shall enjoy so high a power,
That mercy shall be banish'd from our sword;
For we will put each mother's son to death,
And lay thy cities level with the ground:
So will we quench the sparkle that is left
Of thy false son! Aye, as the Lord doth live,
We will chastise him; and our English banner
Shall flout the sky, and fan thy people cold.
'Fore God, thy tongue hath cost thee now thy life. [9]

(ELIZABETH *would have left the room.*)

L. L. Stay, Princess, wage not war! A privy grudge
'Twixt such as you, most high in majesty,
Afflicts both nocent and the innocent.
How many swords, dread Princess, see I drawn—
The friend against his friend, a deadly feud,—
A desperate division in these lands I see!
To God alone belongs revenge;
O, keep those many, many bodies safe
That live and feed upon your majesty;
The single and peculiar life is bound
With all the strength and armour of the mind,
To keep itself from 'noyance; but much more
That Spirit, upon whose spirit depends and rests
The lives of many. The cease of Majesty
Dies not alone but like a gulf doth draw
What's near it, with it. It is a massy wheel
Fixt on the summit of the highest mount,

---

9. "And the incensed Queen would have left, but my father said:—

To whose huge spokes, ten thousand lesser things
Are mortiz'd and adjoin'd which, when it falls,
Each small annexment, petty consequence,
Attends the boist'rous ruin.   Never alone
Did the king sigh, but with a general groan.

  Q. E. Why! how now! dare you speak for this
   'curs'd woman
Who dares to claim the English crown?

  L. L. Dread monarch, this is but a lunacy,
Which grief hath brought this woman to.

  Q. E. False peer,   ·
Thy father was a traitor to the crown,
And thou art traitor to the crown!
In foll'wing this usurping Queen,
Belike thou, too, aspire to the crown,
But neither thou, nor he that loves thee best,
The proudest he that holdest up this doll,
Dare stir a wing, if Elizabeth shake her bells.
I'll have more lives for this
Than drops of blood were in my mother's veins!
How she held up the bill, the neb to thee,
And arm'd her with the boldness of a wife
To her allowing husband!   Already
Inch thick, knee deep, o'er head and ears in love!
Blunt witted lord, ignoble in demeanor,
Every word thou speak'st in her behalf,
Is slander to our royal dignity.
Come woman, kneel and do us homage,
Or, by heaven we swear
We'll force thee do it, maugre all thy pride!
Oh we have physic for a fool!
Pills for a traitor that doth wrong his sovereign!

Most holy and religious fear, will we
Ourselves, provide for thy interious hatred.
What hand made thee, thou proud, ambitious man?
Who gave thee, thou detestable villain,
Thy coronet?   Nay, think thou; thy renown,
Thy orient pearls, thy dear bought movables,
Thy jewels and thy treasure comes from us,
And yet thou makest great account, my lord,
O' th' curs'd usurper who doth defame us,
And hath conspir'd with the French king to kill us.
This man hath eat bread from our royal hand—
This hand hath made him proud with clapping him—
Yet notwithstanding, he would commit
All unlawful actions, contemning God and men,
Friends and country, and all for this lovely leman.
There is no truth or justice to be found in men!
When they are poor and needy, they seek riches;
And when they have them, they covet princely royalty
And hold their manhoods cheap.
Sir, when thou wast ready to be starv'd,
A silly and contemptible sloven,
Ragged in coat and in thy whole apparel,
Did we not load thee with our grace and princely care!
Have we not made thee Master of the Horse,
Besides the most remark'd man i' th' kingdom?
We have with more preferments pursued thee
Than can be well remember'd.   Yet, behold!
Thou dost demand this very, very, fair
Sweet Queen to be thy pillow!   Oh, how sweet
A plant is this that thou hast cropt!   Thine eyes
We thought, did prophesy a royal marriage!
Aye, my lord, all thy knavery we witness'd:

If with this thing it be thou art in love,
Thou shalt have her; we'll gratify thy worth;
We give her frankly unto thee forever,
And ye shall both rake hell for company :
Yet we have heard it in a proverb said :—

> " He that is old and marries with a lass,
> Lies but at home and proves himself an asse."

See her wither'd face, deform'd, diseased; cankered com-
      plexion;
She hath a rotten carcass, viperous mind and epicurean soul:
We pray thee take her; if thou complainest,
By our crown, we swear,
By jarring torture will we cut thee off.
Yea, thou shalt die; for if upon the earth
Any man doth deserve to lose his head,
My lord, thou art that man. [10]

    L. L. God save your majesty; never I am sure,
Have I unto your majesty giv'n cause
To treat me thus: nothing o' th' sort hath happen'd here.
And if it please your majesty to speak,
I do beseech you, madam, to discover
The special cause why you let slip
Such dreadful pudder o'er our heads.
I confess, in sober sadness, marriage is a bondage,
A yoke, a thraldom and a hindrance, too,
To all good enterprises; (this you know)
And this illustrious princess and myself
No such intent could have. On my head fall the blame
And not on hers, if I was half the wooer. [11]

---

10. " My father said :—
11. " With which words, he excited such excessive jealousy
and alarm in my mother that she broke forth into a passionate
speech :—

Q. E. Oh, thou liest! I will prove it on thy heart.
I say thou art enamour'd of this lady,—
This silken-coated, honey-tongued jade.
Oh, I want friends; I am alone, alone!
I am a poor servant; what shall I do? [12]

(ELIZABETH *laughs and weeps.*)

L. L. Oh, I beseech you, madam, pardon me!
For Heaven's sake pardon! See, a beggar begs,
That never begg'd before; love and not fear
Begets my penitence; my happiness
Is in that love, and it doth harrow me
With pain when you, our kingdom's pearl, sit weeping;
But I am crownèd with all joys of love,
When you, O goddess, banish tears away.
Come, madam, come; take me out of the grave;
You are a soul in bliss, but I in desire am bound;
I pray you, madam, speak to your poor knight;
I do beseech your grace to pardon me.

Q. E. Thou perjur'd man,
Scotland's beauty doth stale thy heart,
So go with thy fair love and share her jail. [13]

L. L. If you did love me, as I do you
Thus cruelly you would not let me die,
Devourèd in my love; within this place,
If you pardon me not, and trust me not,

___

12. "My mother did, with this, laugh and then wept with grief; such stores of tears she forth did pour, as if she all to water would have gone; when my father saw her sad stower and how she did weep and wail and make exceeding moan, he, descending from his stage-like greatness, said:—

13. "This made him quickly reinforce his speech, and her beseech, in humble manner, thus:—

I'll die: but what a fool am I, to talk
Of pardon, for your majesty, I know,
Will let me pine away with grief and care!
What have I ever done but love you, Queen?
And yet, I am content the world shall see
How well, if needs, an English earl can die.
Here to your grace, I do bequeath my lands,
My castles, and what holds of me in chief,
And I put your grace in full possession.
If that your grace will not poor Robin pardon,
I am content, for then, you will promise me
The remnant of my fortune to enjoy. [14]

(ELIZABETH *laughs in his face.*)

Q. E. Nay, nay, my lord! this shall not hedge us out.
No, thou ill-nurtured, sly and bloody man!
Thou art blunt of speech, and in conclusion hasty
So blame us not if we do trust thee not.
No, no, sir, we heard her hail thee king,
And we did hidden stand and watch thy pleasure.
Thou slave! down on thy knees and tremble!
Thou caitiff! We will shake thee to pieces. [15]

L. L. Alack, alack! pity me, God!
I am a man more sinn'd against than sinning.
Let the great gods observe my soul, and if
I do not love you with a goodly, cordial love,
Let them unkennel on my naked head
The thunderbolt, that, with sulphur chargèd,
Through the wide cheeks a' th' air doth rive the oak.
Great sovereign, you believe me not;

14. "In high despight, the Queen laughed in his face and said:—
15. "My lord at this cried out:—

Against me you have conceived displeasure,
Yet I love you with a precedent passion,
And witness, Heaven, how dear you are to me. [16]
                    (ELIZABETH *smiles and speaks him fair.*)

  Q. E. I would entreat you, Robin, speak three wise
      words,
For I promise you, none have you spoken here.
I'll freely pardon you after death;
Therefore, speak no more.
I'm sorry you unto this traitor, base,
Have given ear, but as you, willingly,
And of your own accord, have concluded thus
A league between you, I sir, will requite you,
And cut your vital thread in twain. [17]

  L. L. Madam, my sovereign,
Long and happy be your days!
If it please your majesty, give consent
To straight dispatch me, as it sorteth not with me
To live in pain of your perpetual displeasure.
My heart will break! How I may be censured
That nature thus gives way to loyalty,
Something fears me to think; but I prefer
The freedom of divine liberty, more
Than the mortality of imprisonment.
Therefore, as I am bound to die, let me
Die here, where my judge is present;
The gods of heaven forbid that I should e'er
Desire, or wish you to yield your crown to me.

  Q. E. And wherefore, then, did you debate tihs
      business? Speak!

----

16. "So he whined and roared away, until the witty Queen
smiled and spoke him fair:—

17. "He answered:—

L. L. For to espy this lady's own intent,
And do a service to your grace.

    Q. E. Perhaps!
'Tis bravely spoke, and yet I like it not
That you make choice of friends, that hope to trip me:
My lord you have deservèd death, but I
Will pardon you. If you could e'er find out
A country, where but women were that had
Receivèd so much shame, you might begin
A new nation.

    L. L. I thank your majesty.

    Q. E. Hark, sir! speak not! Await you my good
        pleasure.
Good Princess Mary, art thou dumb, or doth
My presence so perturb thy mind, that thou
With a prophetic spirit, do divine
Thy downfall? Nay, nay, Princess, lament not,
He shall enjoy his life and shall abide in safety.
Aye, noble madam, though he hath indeed,
Trimm'd up thy praises with a princely tongue,
Spoke thy deserving like a chronicle,
But still dispraising praise, valued with thee,
Which became him not; yet, because he is
My husband and the father of my sons,
And, withal, loves thee not, I'll pardon him:
But thee I'll bring to justice, thou proud forkèd one,
I'll have thee presently dispatch'd. Thy speech
May not be wash'd in Lethe and forgotten.
My lord, go take her back, and let her not escape;
If she, who for the grave is mark'd, should fly,
I surely will behead thee. Dost thou hear?
Use diligence, therefore, in her return.

Post speedily!   Farewell.

    Q. M. Farewell, proud Queen;
You wrong my lord—my honorable friend—
And, with dishonor to yourself, between
Compulsion and respect, do offer him
The honour of marriage with me.   Is he childish
In reason?   Has he a white beard?   Lies he
Bed-rid?   Or has he grown incapable?
Again, being old, does he dispute his own
Estate?   If not, then why should he not choose
Himself a wife?   This land is mine, and I,
With honor and respect, offer him
These territories, for this day's princely service done
To Scotland, and will make him
My husband without asking your good will;
E'en at your door, I will, with my good lords,
And harness'd troops revel in your nation's chambers.
Sorry am I that you are so old!
I'll have you, England's sometime queen, as you
Affect a sheep's hook, married to my shepherd,
And you shall milk my ewes and weep.   Farewell. [18]
        (ELIZABETH *smiles and drops Mary a curtsie.*

    Q. E. Then thou compell'st this Prince to wear the
        crown?
But, sir, how often shall I bid thee bear her hence?

    L. L. Come wend with me, and we will leave. [19]

    Q. M. Let me but stay and speak; I will not go.

    L. L. Come, come away!
I pray you give me leave to lead you forth.

---

    18. "The Queen did smile at this, and, with excellent cour-
tesy, said :—

    19. "Said my lord:—

Q. M. Back, sir; lay not your hand on me!
I wonder much that you, a mighty man,
Should be a traitor unto me, your Queen;
'Tis more than God or man will well allow.
    L. L. Come.
    Q. M. Oh, let me live! Set down my ransom!
King James will make it good.
    L. L. Pray, speak no more.
I beseech your grace to return with me;
Come, and if I live, I will promise
Not to bewray you, but ere the sunset,
To see you plac'd safely in the castle
From whence you came original.
    Q. M. Oh! your desert speaks loud, and I should
        wrong it
To lock it in the wards of covert bosom,
When it deserves, with character of brass,
A forted residence 'gainst the tooth of time,
And razure of oblivion! My faith, my lord,
In your integrity stands without blemish.
    L. L. Now is your time; give me your hand; kneel
Before Elizabeth and pray for mercy.
    Q. M. You bid me seek redemption of the devil.
If I would speak, she'd mock me into air;
Oh! she would laugh me out o' myself; press me
To death with wit: therefore let the old witch,
The hag—who's neither maid, widow, nor wife,—
With all ill-meaning, spill my blood.
I will not trouble more with gentle words,

20. "There she stopped, with tears; her swollen heart her
speech seemed to bereave. The Queen, with fell look and
hollow deadly gaze, stared on her: while, as one astound, my
lord not one word had to speak, and, by outward signs, showed
his great amaze:—

This degenerate bastard of a strumpet mother. [20]

(MARY stops with tears.)

My lord, my lord, thou cruel lord!
What frayes ye, that were wont to comfort me?
Of this vile strumpet art thou then afraid?
She, who on my life doth feed—who sucks the blood,
Which from my heart doth bleed!   Confess the truth,
And say by whose advice I here did come.
Thou dost smile at this, Lord Robert.

    L. L. By my troth, thou speakest truth! the Queen,
Conceiving great fear of my frail safety,
Will'd me to bring thee here.

    Q. M. O, you most blessèd ministers above,
Keep me in patience, and with ripen'd time
Unfold the evil, which is here wrapt up
In countenance.   Look you, my lord, did you
As you've confess'd, know that within this chamber,
Her highness was conceal'd?   Is it true?

    L. L. It is true.

    Q. M. O hear me, Justice,—

    L. L. Oh, heavens! the vanity
Of wretched fools! oh, hear her not, your highness,
For she will speak most bitterly and strange!

    Q. M. Most strange, but yet most truly will I speak,
That Leicester is foresworn; is it not strange?
That Robert is a murderer, is't not strange?
That Dudley is an adulterous thief,
An hypocrite, a virgin-violator,
Is it not strange, and strange?

    Q. E. Nay, it is ten times strange.

    Q. M. Then this is all as true as it is strange:
Nay, it is ten times true, for truth is truth

To the end of reckoning.

    Q. E. Away with her! Poor soul,
She speaks this in th' infirmity of sense.

    Q. M. I conjure thee, as thou believest
There is another comfort than this world,
That thou neglect me not with that opinion
That I am touch'd with madness: make not impossible
That which but seems unlike; 'tis not impossible
But one, the wicked'st caitiff on the ground,
May seem as shy, as grave, as just, as absolute
As he; even so may he, your majesty,
In all his dressings, caracts, titles, forms,
Be an arch-villain: believe it, royal Princess
If he be less, he's nothing, but he's more,
Had I more name for badness.

    L. L. Darkness and devils! saddle my horses;
Call my train together. By mine honesty,
If she be mad, as I believe no other
From these idle words, 'tis time she were away.

    Q. E. Away with her; she is a courtesan,
And truly will devise some villainous slander
To stain and impoison you, my lord. I'll curb
Her mad and headstrong humour and give her justice.

    Q. M. Lead me whither thou wilt, even to my death.
I have, my lord, heard much of thy hospitality,
But I see, this Queen, that the kingly sceptre bears,
Resting in jealous dread, thinks best
To remove me somewhere away.
Prepare my horses, marble-hearted friend—
More hideous than the sea-monster—
I'll strive no longer, but will follow thee:
Come, come, away! I'll follow thee, my lord,

Unto my prison, where I may wail and weep
All that I may. Give leave, madam,
That these slaves of thine may take me to my death.

    Q. E. Go! feed not thyself with fond persuasion.
Assuredly thou shalt not a succession
Or a successor upon us impose.

    Q. M. I know not that, but of this I am assur'd,
That death ends all, and I can die but once!
Leicester, farewell.

    L. L. Not yet, your grace, I'll bear you on your way.

    Q. E. Stop, my lord, this must not be!
Thou may'st not take this railer into Shrewsbury.
Where are the warriors brave, that with this plague
Did come? Let them amain towards Shrewsbury march,
And take this great-grown traitor with them:
Hence with her! Come, sir, thou must walk by us,
While we do bend our course unto the Tower;
After this night's perilous task, good supporters must we
      have,
On other hand, our soldiers that are below.
Come, sir, away! Farewell, thou plague. [21]
(ELIZABETH *starts to leave, leaning on the shoulder of* LEICES-
    TER—MARY *springs from her seat.*)

    Q. M. My lord, I tell you that you're a base-born
And abject swain, and weel I wot, you seem
Like to the almanac of the old year with the new.
You coward! to save your paltry life you have made
Me smart. Surely, all the glory you have won

---

    21. "And the ruthless, unrelenting Queen would have left
the poor, foolish and pernicious woman sitting on the floor.
As soon as she beheld the Queen pass, leaning on the shoulder
of his lordship, from the ground lightly upstarting, she did
begin, with nods and smiles to scorn him:—

By your insulting tyranny is guilty shame.
Oh, monstrous treachery, can this be so
Thàt in alliance, amity and oaths,
There should be found such false, dissembling guile?
Life's sweet to me: oh, shame to you, base knight!
You dastard, that before a stroke is given,
Like to a coward squire doth run away!
For your malicious practices, your foes
Should tear the garter from your craven leg,
Because unworthily you are install'd
In that high degree.   Such cowards as you, I vow,
Ought not to wear that ornament of knighthood:
Yea, when the truth is known, the world will say,
That I was thus surpris'd, was infamous,
And ill-beseeming any man, in fact,
Much more a knight, a captain, and a leader.
When first this Order was ordained,
Knights of the Garter were of noble birth;
Valiant and virtuous, full of haughty courage,
Such as were grown to credit by the wars:
Not fearing death nor shrinking for distress,
But always resolute in most extremes:
He then, that is not furnish'd in this sort,
Doth but usurp the sacred name of knight,
Profaning this most honorable Order,
And should, if I were worthy to be judge,
Be quite degraded, like a hedge-born swain,
That doth presume to boast of gentle blood.
Ignoble lord, stain to your countrymen,
Follow, I pray, your desperate paramour,
As Icarus did of old his sire of Crete;
Yet, what a peevish fool was that of Crete

That taught his son the office of a fowl!
Indeed, for all his wings the fool was drown'd:
Rather am I Dædalus; you, the poor boy
Icarus; and she, the sun that scared
The wings of that sweet boy, or else the sea,
Whose envious gulf did swallow up his life.
Sure am I, sir, you are well kiss'd, and that
She will dissolve you yet: her sister slew
The Earl of Northumberland, your father,
And, coupled in bonds of perpetuity,
Two Dudleys, soon, will through the lither sky
Have wing'd their flight. [22]
                                    (ELIZABETH *laughs in scorn.*)

  Q. E. Lo, my dear lord,
These words of hers draw life-blood from our heart!
Art weary of thy life? If thou dost make us stay,
'Tis but the shortening of thy life one day!
Thou hear'st thy doom; be packing, therefore, straight;
Thou tempt'st the fury of our three attendants—
Lean famine, quartering steel and climbing fire:
Thou ominous and fearful owl of death,
Thy nation's terror and their bloody scourge,
The period of thy tyranny approaches.
Moved with compassion of thy country's wrack,
Together with the pitiful complaints
Of such as thy oppression feeds upon,
We have, upon a special cause, concluded
To root thee up, and spill the base,
Contaminated, misbegotten blood
Of thine that is polluted with thy lusts,
Stain'd with the guiltless blood of innocents,

---

22. " Here Elizabeth laughed in scorn and said:-

Corrupt and tainted with a thousand vices:
And then, with colours spread to march
With all our English troops following after us,
To lay thy stately, air-braving towers even with the earth,
And give unto thy son chastisement for this abuse,
And let him perceive how ill we brook his mother's
    treason.
My lord, take leave of this fair giglot wench;
Come, side by side together will we leave.

    Q. M. Go; do what you will! I command you, go!
Flight shall not clear you from this murd'rous stain!
No more can I be sever'd from your side,
No more can you yourselves in twain divide.

        (*The* EARL'S *servants form a lane,*
            through which the QUEENS *make exit.*) [23]

---

   23. "At the Queen's going away, the Earl's servants stood in a seemly manner in their livery coats, and cognizancies, ranged on both sides, and made the Queen a lane; then forth, through the city to the Tower gates, they marched; from whence, unto the valiant Earl of Shrewsbury, their fair prisoner was straight dispatched.

(Bacon and the Decipherer.)

" Now sir, if you, the writer of this narrative, will again read o'er the lines, you will see that I have changed my style, and compiled this tragic history as a play, and, act by act, tell the event."

" How many acts are there?"

" Five, wherein I purpose to speak actively, without dilating or digressing. Turn backward, and single out the play and the players."

" What am I to do when I find out where the tragedy begins?"

" Bring it forth. Faithfully transcribed, it discloses the author of the plays, because, if I, Master Francis Bacon, set down the history of my father, my mother, and the Queen of Scots, as a play, and did mask it in plays, then I did write them all. In my judgment, though some may speak openly against my books, when they come to read the play—which is of a self-same colour as King John, Henry the Fourth, Henry the Fifth, and Henry the Sixth on the one side, and Cæsar, Othello, and the Comedies on the other,—it will prove me, Francis Bacon, to have been the author of these narrations, and satisfy the mountebanks, that represent you as full of knavish impostures. When your auditors hear and see this play, in which are lines, that with the most excellent of the others are parallel, they will leave no sour annoy for you. Even the youths that thunder at a play-house will, with their loud applause and aves vehement, cut off all ill-affected speech. And here, I hope, begins your lasting joy; aye, in my heart of hearts I do; for behold! you, yourself, do take a taking part."

" What's here? I take no part in this, but that of the maid's—I dance to another's music."

" Not so. One scene of it, you will find, is Bacon with his scholar; the lines his pupil speaks are no other than the

Cipher's key; that part is yours, and so, you shall convert the world to single thinking, with your own voice."

" I love the people, but I do not like to stage me to their eyes. Though it do well, I do not relish well this childish sport; I will not represent my own image."

" Well then, let me speak."

" I stay upon your leisure."

"O stand forth, and, with bold spirit, relate what you, most like a careful subject, have collected out of my misplac'd books. Speak it, as I pronounce it to you, trippingly on the tongue: if you mouth it, as many players do, I had as leave the town crier spoke my lines. Do not saw the air too much with your hand, thus, but use all gently: for you must acquire and beget a temperance. Now, my lord, I desire to give you, by parallels, the secret that deludes them all."

" It is impossible."

" I say nay to that, my lord, I know that you are a king of learning, and that, prompted and incited by the nature of your education, you have done the work of a servant, and yet thereby your well-deserved Honour and Reputation is certain. No doubt, without your eyes, these stories, (disclosing the greatest mysteries of this Isle,) could never have been resolved; but now you will bring to a happy issue, the exact solution of my riddle, which argues your wisdom and your love. And, I hope good Fortune, will give you hours of happiness without number; and that, wearing the garland I have presented you, you will take your place on the seat of the poets; and I hope your name will go with mine through all ages. Your scope is as mine own, so to enforce the laws as to your soul seems good. May the heavens give safety to your purposes; and, to the hopeful execution of your commission do I leave you. Once more, give me your hand, and I'll lead you forth and bring you back in safety. Take my blessing; God protect you, into whose hands I give my life. Fare you well."

" I thank you. Farewell."

Actus Secundus. Scena Prima.

(Street in front of the Tower gates, London. Time, midnight.)
Enter QUEEN ELIZABETH, EARL OF LEICESTER *and train, with torches.*

Q. E. My lord,
Nobly and sumptuously hast thou entertain'd .
This fair rebel.   Oh, how much art thou like
Mark Antony, who kiss'd his orient pearl
With many double kisses!
And thou, my brave Mark Antony, hast
In immodest love, with many a joyful kiss
And melting tear, embraced this vain castaway,
" Whose flow'ring pride, so fading and so fickle,
    Short Time shall soon cut down with his consuming sickle. "
High-minded Cleopatra, sovereign of Egypt,
With stroke of asp did sting herself to death;
And Sthenebœa bold, with wilful cord
Did choke herself for wanting of her will;
But thou false knave, this worthless mistress o' thine,
Can do no more than backbite my good name.
Ha! hie thee home to bed,
Thou subtile, perjur'd, false, disloyal man.
Think'st thou I am so shallow, so conceitless,
To be seducèd by thy flattery?
Thou hast deceiv'd so many with thy vows,
That thou thinkest thou art sure of me.
Thy bones are hollow, and impiety
Hath made a feast of thee; which of thy hips,
Has, sir, the most profound sciatica?
Nay, but I know thee; I am priz'd so slight
That thou hast forsworn me thus shamelessly.

Think'st thou thy oaths will compass thy least wish?
Though each particular saint they would swear down,
My good lord, I would not now believe them.
Oh! I have fed upon this woe, already,
And now excess of it will make me surfeit;
Even as one heat another heat expels,
Or as one nail by strength drives out another,
So the remembrance of thy former love
Is by a newer object quite forgotten.
Nay, more;
All th' cunning manner of my death's determin'd of,
And all the means are plotted and 'greed on:
I know how she must from her window climb,
At th' midnight hour, and that thou, for her flight,
Will have all necessaries that she must use,—
The ladder of cord is made, and now is in
The chamber of mine enemy. Believe me,
Were I of evil disposition, sir,
Within three days thy head would be chopp'd off;
But after all, I am in this, thy wife,
And at the hazard of my friends and state,
I'll use thee gently. From henceforth, from me
And from thy friends, my lord, thou art banish'd;
Thy falsehood, cowardice and poor descent—
Three things that women highly hold in hate—
I will forget, and in dumb silence bury
The slander and the shame thou'st put on me;
And now begone; I'll presently deliver
Thee thy commission. [24]

24. "The Earl, when great Cynthia's displeasure brake,
with wonderous skill did plain, and move for her to take him
to her grace again; said he:—

L. L. You are void of pity,
If you do banish me. O pity me,
My love, and pardon me, sweet Queen!

Q. E. My stubborn smart
Thou dost not aught assuage, but more annoyance breed.
Therefore, speak not! Thy best appointment make with
        speed,—
To-morrow you set on. Go! Fare thee well.

L. L. Is there no remedy?

Q. E. None but such remedy
As, to save a head, to cleave a heart in twain.

L. L. But is there any?

Q. E. Yes, there's a devilish mercy in thy judge
If thou wilt implore it, that will free thee
From banishment, but it will fetter thee till death.

L. L. Perpetual durance?

Q. E. Aye, just perpetual durance;
A restraint through all the world's vastidity.

L. L. Oh! I do fear thee, and I quake!
O let me entreat thee cease. Give me thy hand,
That I may dew it with my mournful tears;
Nor let the rain of heaven wet this place,
To wash away my woful monument.
Oh, could this kiss be printed in thy hand,
That thou mightest think upon the seal,
Through whom a thousand sighs are breath'd for thee!

Q. E. Get thee gone! Speak not to me! Even now,
        begone!

L. L. Oh, go not yet; even thus two friends con-
        demn'd,
Embrace and kiss and take ten thousand leaves,
Loather a hundred times to part, than die:

Yet now farewell, and farewell life with thee;
Thus is poor Robin ten times banishèd—
Once by his fault, and three times thrice by thee. [25]

(Elizabeth *thrusts him away,*
enters the palace gates, which close.)

I'll empty all these veins, and drop by drop,
Shed my dear blood in' th' earth, ere I will go!
Let my soul want mercy, if I do not join
In her behalf with Scotland! She is fair,
And not a scurvy, old cozening devil,
Who, like the sanctimonious pirate
That went to sea with the ten commandments,
Scrap'd out of the table—" Thou shalt not steal;"
I have heard that her grace, hath razed
A commandment to leave her free.
God-a-mercy! If I do speak or laugh
Familiarly with such or such woman,
Then presently she is, without a cause,
So jealous and suspicious, that she doth
Vulgarly and personally let slip,
Even like an o'ergrown lion in a cave,
That goeth out to prey.

  F. Bacon. But she loves you,
And love, you know, is full of jealousy.

   L. L. What! what fellow was that that dared to
    speak?

   F. B. My lord, 'twas I.

   L. L. What man art thou?

---

25. "She would not hear and stoutly thrust him away.
and did enter in the tower gates; when my lord saw that all
hope was gone, and all that he had foolishly lost by game of
tick-tack, he did unloose his tied-up tongue and damned the
woman that wronged him; he said:—

F. B. Son to your noble lordship.

L. L. Well done, my boy. What hath called thee
here?

F. B. I came to see thyself.

L. L. What seek ye, Francis?

F. B. My lord, cheer up your heart. Your foes are
nigh,

And this soft courage makes your followers faint.

L. L. Hold, villain! hold! Should I suspect
Thou wouldst betray me, I would murder thee.

F. B. I am too mean a subject for thy wrath;
Upon her grace, be thou reveng'd and let me live;
But kill me with thy weapon, not with words,
Or, rather, use thy sword to rid thee of thy foes;
My breast can better brook thy dagger's point,
Than can my ears, among this company,
Hear thee so make our gracious Queen thy theme!
If thou please, let us hence, and thus avoid
Her ill-timed suspicion. Bitter fear
O'er-shades me; it is folly, in the streets
So to babble and talk. Thy fingers to thy lips,
And I will respect thee as a father,
But thy discretion better can persuade,
Than I am able to instruct or teach;
Therefore let us go cheerfully together,
And digest thy angry choler on thine enemies.
If thou forsake our gracious Queen,
To waste thyself upon a fugitive,
Thou art not worthy, sir, of preservation.

L. L. Boy, by my soul, she knew not what she did
When thus she spake to me. Knowest thou
That I am banished? Ah! hadst thou heard

Her foul reproaches, full deeply then,
Thou hadst divin'd my unqualitied shame.

    F. B. My lord, I have heard and seen all.

    L. L. Well then,
Should I not ease my heart, even if it be
With hazard of my head? I prithee, boy,
Trouble me no more.

    F. B. What valor were it, when a cur doth grin,
For one to thrust his hand between his teeth,
When he might spurn him with his foot away?
To take all vantages, is no impeach
Of valor, sir. What would your lordship do?
Make stand against the Queen?
My lord, so strives the woodcock with the gynne,
So doth the connie struggle in the net.

    L. L. So triumph thieves upon their conquer'd booty.

    F. B. So true men yield, with robbers so o'ermatcht.
Wrath makes you deaf; you talk like one that doth
Upon a mole-hill stand, and reach with outstretcht arms,
At rocky mountains, yet, when all is done,
Hath parted but the shadow with his hand.
Come, your father's, Northumberland's, head—
After many scorns, many foul taunts—they took,
And on the gates they set the same, and there
It did remain, the saddest spectacle
That ere was view'd: and, ten to one, she'll do
To you as was unto Northumberland done.

    L. L. I know it well; yet blame me not.
She forbade my tongue to speak, and boy,
I' th' presence of my servants, aye, with outstretcht throat,
Did tell the world aloud my privy faults.

    F. B. The fox barks not, when he would steal the lamb;

Dismiss your followers and abate your wrath.
I grant that oft she puts her tongue to speech
Not fit for Albion's sovereign; but for you,
My lord, it had been better you had kiss'd
Your three fingers, than with your tongue to tell
The passion of your heart.   She is your Queen,
And heedful ears may chance to find you out;
Then will thick darkness and the gloomy shade
Of death environ you, till mischief and despair
Drive you to break your neck, or hang yourself.

  L. L. Peace, peace!
Boiling choler chokes the passage of my voice!
I'll plant the Scottish Queen even in the chair of state.
This answer (at my dearest cost) I will
Return to her.

  F. B. My gracious lord, the cedar,
Whose arms give shelter to the princely eagle,
Under whose shade the ramping lion sleeps,
Whose top-branch overpeers Jove's spreading tree,
And keeps low shrubs from Winter's powerful wind,
Yields to the axe's edge: those eyes,
That now are piercing as the mid-day sun
To search the secrets of the world,
Will then be dimm'd with death's black veil;
The wrinkles on your brows, which have been liken'd oft
To kingly sepulchres, with blood be fill'd;
Your glory smear'd in dust and blood; your parks,
Your walks, your manors, be delivered
Unto your foes; and of all your lands,
Naught will be left but your poor body's length.
Dig not your grave! turn not to earth and dust!
Away, away! live, rule and reign!

Turn th' leaf and read, and in the interim,
Having weigh'd it, recover all your loss again.
Think what hath chanc'd, is but new honors come
Upon you, which like to strange garments, fit
Not to their mould but with the aid of use.
Be patient, good my lord, cease to lament.

    L. L. Thy speech shows fair; be thou my advocate
With the angry Queen.

    F. B. What would you have me plead for, my lord?

    L. L. As thou lovest and tenderest me,
Dissuade the Queen from having me banish'd.
Oh! banished!—that one word—banished!
It presses to my memory,
Like evil deeds to dying sinners' minds!
Plead for me that I be not exiled.

    F. B. My lord, your lordship knows, it lies
Not in my power to dissuade the Queen;
But I will testify my zeal unto the crown,
And, as I bear your name, with show of zeal
Will speak in your behalf. Why look you still
So stern and tragical?

    L. L. Thou wilt be repuls'd.

    F. B. It may be very likely; but I hope
That words, sweetly placed and modestly directed,
Will change her mind and save you from exile.
Come, my lord, break not now into passion,
But speak her fair and flatter, most obsequious
And willing.

    L. L. Knowing how hardly I can brook abuse,
It is not well, thus boldly to whip me!
Yet I, in silence, will keep in, and if
There yet remains of thy persuading art

A little remnant, why, appease, I pray,
Our jealous Queen.

  F. B. My lord, I will plead well
Your fair deserts, and be assur'd I will
Repeal you, or adventure to be banished
Myself. But look, my lord, our torches die.

  L. L. Do not light them.
I'll lock thy worthy counsel in my breast,
And what I do imagine, let it rest.   (*Exeunt.*)

Scena Secunda.

(*Audience Room of the Palace.*)
QUEEN ELIZABETH *and* MASTER FRANCIS BACON.

  Queen Elizabeth. Well pleadest thou, for this great
   peer,
But tell me, sith that thou and I are here,
How is't t' enrich the storehouse of thy powerful wit,
That this great bagpipe man, that roars so loud
And thunders in the night, comes not himself?

  Francis Bacon. He hath sent me in his stead, and
As did Aeneas old Anchises bear,
So bear I, upon my manly shoulders,
My father's fame; but Aeneas bare a living load,
Nothing so heavy as these woes of his.
Uncurable discomfit reigns within
His heart, and he doth entreat your grace, that
Have into monstrous habits put the graces
That once were his, with charity to interpret

His well-disposèd mind; and weeping forth
His welcomes, asks of thee forgiveness.

  Q. E. Hark! dare not speak too loud, lest that thy
   speech
Shall to our flaming wrath be oil and flax.
We will not have to do with pity.
The well-disposèd mind growing once corrupt,
Turns noble benefits to vicious forms,
Ten times more ugly than ever they were fair.
This man so complete, who was enroll'd 'mongst wonders,
That when he spoke, we almost with ravish'd list'ning,
Could not find his hour of speech, a minute;
He, fit indeed to use in all assays—
Whether for arms and warlike amenaunce,
Or for a wise and civil governaunce—
Doth, in his courting of this strange princess,
Invite us aye, to act in cruelty.
Into as many gobbits will we cut
That fatal screech-owl to our house,—
That nothing sings but death to us and ours,—
As wild Medea, young Abisirtis did.
Death will stop her dismal threatening sound,
And her ill-boding tongue no more shall speak:
Dark cloudy death will overshade her beams of life;
And we'll surely blast thy father's harvest.
Take heed lest that sweet Death doth reap thee, too!
We'll banish him on pain of death.

  F. B. Forgive my presumption.

  Q. E. Hadst thou been kill'd when first thou didst
   presume,
Thou hadst not liv'd to be attorney
For this base ignoble wretch.

God knows thou art the first fruit of my flesh,
But hast thy father's heart.   Thy parentage
Thou canst not e'er deny, fill'd as thou art
With all thy father's vicious qualities:
I did bear thee, but he did beget thee.
Begone, thou graceless boy! get thee from my sight.

    F. B. Here on my knee, I beg mortality
Rather than life preferr'd with infamy!
If I, to-day, die not with thy fell rage,
To-morrow I shall die with mickle age!
That my father might be saved, to thee I come;
O twice my mother, twice am I thy son;
Thou gav'st me life, and rescued me from death,
I give to thee my sword, my soul, my breath;
Rather than ill shall shame my mother's womb,
All my fair hopes shall lie in one dark tomb:
No power have I to speak for him, I know,
And so farewell.   I and my griefs will go.

                             (Enter a messenger.)

    Mess. Your grace, the Earl of Leicester
Doth crave to be admitted to your presence.

    Q. E. What means his grace, that he so plain and
        blunt
Doth audience demand?   Let him come near.

                             (Enter Leicester.)

I' God's name, lord, how darest thou attend on us?
Go home; return unto thy house; there bow
Thy stubborn knees and pray for her whom thou
Hast vow'd to serve.

    Leicester. I am the wofullest man that ever liv'd,
For I in oblivion and hateful griefs
Must live.   Dearer than life art thou to me!

Now my soul's palace is become a prison;
Ah! would it break from hence, that this, my body,
Might in the ground be closèd up in rest:
For never, henceforth, shall I joy again,
Never, oh, never shall I see more joy!
To thee I pray, sweet Queen, O pity me
Before I take my death!   I never did thee harm!
Why wilt thou slay me?

    Q. E. Silence thine idle tongue!   I'll set thee up a
      glass,
Where thou mayst see the inmost part of thee.
Lay not the flatt'ring unction to thy soul,
That not thy trespass but my anger speaks:
It will but skin and film the ulcerous place,
Whilst rank corruption, mining all within,
Infects unseen.   Confess thyself to heaven;
Repent what's past; avoid what is to come;
And do not spread the compost on the weeds,
To make them rank.   Sir, I saw the wanton
Pinch thy cheek, call thee her mouse, and slyly,
Whilst paddling in thy neck with her damn'd fingers,
Give thee a pair of reehie kisses.
Had I her brethren here, their lives and hers
Were not revenge sufficient for me:
No, if I digg'd up her forefathers' graves,
And hung their rotten coffins up in chains,
It could not slake mine ire, nor ease my heart.
The sight of her or any of her house,
Is as a fury to torment my soul;
Until I root out her accursed line
And leave not one alive, I live in hell.
Therefore, begone.

L. L. O thou hast cleft my heart in twain.

Q. E. O throw away the worser part of it,
And live the purer with the other half.
Thou hast out-paramour'd the Turk.

L. L. Your highness, it is no blot or foulness,
No unchaste action or dishonor'd step,
That hath depriv'd me of thy grace and favor.
It is but this: that jealous of my love,
To work my fortune's ill with foul suspicion,
The gallants stuff thy ears,—
Oh! monstrous villainy,—when they know
Sooner would I the fiery elements
Dissolve, and make thy kingdom in the sky,
Than this base earth should shroud your majesty.

Q. E. I bear an honourable mind, and am
Not carried with the common wind of courts,
Nor do I after tattling fables fly.
Restrain thy apprehension; I will lay
Trust upon thee, and thou shalt find I will
Preserve and love thee; I've conferred on thee
The commandment of mine army beyond the sea.
Now, my lord, to the council follow me.

L. L. I will attend upon your highness. [26]   (*Exeunt.*)

---

26. " Unto the council chamber they have gone, thence
will we, therefore, to look on and see, how in their counsels,
they do all agree:—

Actus Tertius. Scena Prima.

(*Council Chamber of the Palace*).
Lords seated at Table. Queen Elizabeth *on a raised throne.*

Queen Elizabeth. My lords, Philip of Spain,—the foul, accursed minister of hell,—hath joined with the Frenchmen, our baleful enemies, and in league with Burgundy, gathers strength. Their armies that were divided into two parts, are now conjoined in one, and presently mean to give battle to the states of Christendom. Moved with remorse of these outrageous broils, we trust the proffer we have made unto the rightful Lord Protector of the Low Countries, will give you all content. This letter doth contain it. This it is. We have begged my lord to accept this, our servant, whom we send as image of our power, to be the captain of our victorious, arm̀d Englishmen, that now war with him against our enemies. Judge then, great lords, if we have done amiss in this. Speak freely, we cannot hear too much in matter of such moment: my good Lord Chancellor, speak thou as free as mountain wind.

Lord Chancellor. Your grace, it is not meet that he should be sent as your grace's image, for that he was a traitor to the crown. His father shook hands with death, and will you pale your head in the son's glory, and rob your temples of the diadem? For he doth hope to reign. He hath gelded the commonwealth, and made of it an eunuch, and should your majesty put about his neck the scarf, and in his hands the staff, no good will come of it.

Lord Leicester. I beseech your majesty, do not cast away an honest man for a villain's accusation.

Q. E. By the eternal God, whose name and power
thou tremblest at, answer what we shall ask.   Thou shalt
not pass from hence but to execution, till thou dost speak
the truth.

L. L. Ask what thou wilt.

Q. E. Think'st thou to rise from beggar's state unto
this princely seat?   Hast thou intent to destroy the realm
and slay your sovereign?

L. L. 'Tis their intent to slaughter me.
Oh, were mine eyeballs into bullets turn'd,
That I, in rage, might shoot them at their faces!
Grant me th' commission, gracious sovereign,
And you may behold confusion of your foes.
So help me righteous God, against this state
I have no thought; with pure, unspotted heart,
Never yet taint with aught but love, I have,
O gentle Princess, ever sought to be
A faithful servant t' mine anointed Queen :
Your grace doth know, it is because no one should sway,—
No one but he, should be about your grace,—
That doth engender thunder in his breast,
And makes him roar his accusations forth ;
But he shall know I am as good as he.

L. C. No, my good lords, it is not that offends,—
It is not that, that hath incensed me!
Thou lordly sir, and what art thou, I pray,
But one imperious in another's throne?
And if thy thoughts were sifted, I fear me
The Queen, thy sovereign, is not quite exempt
From envious malice of thy swelling heart.
For such is thy audacious wickedness,—
Thy lewd, pestif'rous and dissentious pranks,—

As very infants prattle of thy pride.

L. L. I do desire thee, sovereign, and lords,
Vouchsafe to give me hearing what I shall reply.
If I were covetous, ambitious or perverse,
As he will have me, how am I so poor?
Or how haps it I seek not to advance
Or raise myself, but keep my wonted colour?
And for dissensions, who preferreth peace
More than I do—except I be provok'd?
Mark the intent o' this nimble-witted councillor,
Who, in cold considerance hath sentenc'd me!
He knows the game, how true he keeps the wind.

Q. E. Silence! Be patient, lords! Why stand ye on
nice points? My lord Earl, we have made thee Master of
our Forces. Stoop, and bend thy knee. Swear that thou
wilt, whilst thou enjoyest this royal dignity, ease thy
country of distressful war; and though in foreign land,
when dreadful danger feeds his doubtful humour, and is
wont all zeal of justice to cut off, that thou wilt hold up
our warlike sword, and for St. George and victory fight:
and that thou wilt live and die for England's fame, and
be true liegeman to our crown. Take thou thy oath.

L. L. So help me God, I will, your majesty.

Q. E. Take thy commission then, as General of the
    Forces.
Success unto our valiant general,
And happiness to his accomplices.
As time and our concernings importune,
We shall write to thee how it goes with us:
And so, my lord, with all the speed thou mayst,
Set on towards thy commandment.
The justice of the quarrel and the cause,

Much honor will engrave upon thy brows.
This sudden execution of our will,
We know thou wilt excuse, for till thou dost return
We rest perplexed with a thousand cares.
But we, as erst Princess Andromanche,
Seated amidst the crew of Priam's sons,
Have liberty to choose where best we love.
Then be not sad, for 'tis our right,
To name our captain and our knight.[27]   (*Exeunt.*)

Scena Secunda.

(*Council Chamber of Palace, twelve months later.*)
Lords of the Council and QUEEN ELIZABETH.

Queen Elizabeth. Lords, take your places.   Lord
Chamberlain, where are our notes?   Behold, my lords,
the sly conveyances of Scotland's Queen unto Henry King
of France.   She here doth claim our crown by right, and
we pray you all, proceed from this true evidence.   God
forbid any malice should prevail, or that faultless, you
condemn her.   Pray God she may acquit her of suspicion
but if she be approved in practice culpable, then we intend
to try her grace.

---

27. "Now I slide over twelve months space: I turn my
glass, and give my scene such growing, as you had slept
between.   My tale is now about the Lady's death."

"Were your eyes witness of her attainder and her death?"

"No, but I was in the beaten track of that I tell you of."

"Thou soulderest close impossibilities, and make them kiss,
that speakest with every tongue, to every purpose; let us on."

"Good my lord, look then.   Officers and counsellors are
in place.   The Queen begins :—

Lord Chancellor. Great Sovereign, vouchsafe to hear me speak, and let your chancellor's counsel now prevail. I bend my knee against the Queen, that in thus aiming at your life hath tempted judgment. I, and the rest that are your counselors, with a general consent, demand that articles shall forthwith be drawn touching the rank treason of the Queen. Before my God, I might not this believe, without the sensible and true avouch of mine own eyes, but I have viewed these treasonable abuses of her grace, and madam, I would have her, in private, ascend to heaven. Granted scope of speech, will she not swear false allegations to o'erthrow the state? Then let her be sent to heaven, without the acclamations and applauses of the people.

Q. E. Heaven forbid! My lords, at once the care you have of us, to mow down thorns that would annoy our foot is worthy praise. We thank you. These words content us much, but shall we speak our conscience? God forefend that Mary be done to death in secret. There are such proofs of the Queen's treason, letters from the King of France found in her boxes, the bold-faced, bloody, devilish practises upon our life, with many other evidences of deep deceit that proclaim her with all certainty, to be a fox in stealth, false in heart and bloody of hand, but we can give the loser leave to chide; and we will not contrary to law, devise strange death for her; and we heartily beseech you, dishonor not your sovereign: therefore call home again the noble Earl, and in the balance of our English peers, let her be weighed: If she weigh light then she needs must fall. Here are your commissions. And now, my gentle lords, fair duty to you all. Look into the bottom of this troublesome evil, for know,

under our seal we have with special and displayèd mind,
lent you our terror, dressed you with our love, and to you,
given all the organs of our power. We think you will
solemnly bear at full, our grace, honor and wisdom.

L. C. Always obedient to your grace, we will not
warp the ample power that your highness hath possessed
us with, against our oaths and true allegiance sworn.

Q. E. On Thursday next, thou shalt set forward. The
Clerk of the Crown hath begun the penning of your lordships' letters of commission, which are fac-similies of this.
Forty peers, knights, captains, lawyers and gentlemen,
we shall employ to try this o'er-topping woman's treason,
and to dispose of her as they think good. To-night, we
hold our solemn supper, and we request the presence of
our friends.

All. Let your highness command us.

Q. E. God's benyson go with you all.   Farewell. [23]

(*Exeunt.*)

---

28. " In conduct of the Earl of Shrewsbury, the Queen of
Scots had, within the realm of England, been at Coventry,
Wingfield, Sheffield, and. Shrewsbury, but was a short time
before her trial, by will and warrant of our gracious sovereign,
removed to Fotheringay Castle, in Northamptonshire. Of
those summoned to serve, thirty-four answered. My lords of
Derby, Pembroke, Rutland, Worcester, Northumberland,
Shrewsbury, Kent, Lincoln, Oxford, Stafford, Gray and Warwick, the Lord Treasurer, the Knights Montague, Hatton,
Walsingham and many other lords and gentlemen appeared
at the castle, and on the eleventh of the eighth month, and
for some twelve days thereafter, diligently applied themselves
to the cause. The Lord Chancellor called Mary before them,
and as a prisoner she was brought to the bar, and, in view of
the commission, spake to this effect :—

Actus Quartus.   Scena Prima.

(*Room in Fotheringay Castle.*)
Lords, Knights, Captains, Lawyers and Gentlemen in attendance.
QUEEN MARY *at the Bar.*

Queen Mary. My learned lords: there is a fault
amongst you, and I speak it to your shame. I am the
Queen of Scots, and yet none dare speak for me: and further, be it in more shame spoken, the English Queen,
Elizabeth, is not here. Hear then, my resolution: the
French King's sister and mother of the King of Scots,
doth crave the presence of the English Queen.

Lord Chancellor. Madam, our Queen hath, in her
absence, elected us to supply her great countenance and
place; there is our commission.

Q. M. Then hear me, mighty lords, ye wish my ruin:
Is this your Christian counsel?   Out upon ye!
Heaven is above ye all yet; there sits a Judge
That no king can corrupt.
And shall the figure of God's majesty—
His captain, Stewart, deputy elect,
Anointed, crown'd, and planted many years,—
Be judg'd by subject and inferior breath?
Ye turn me into nothing: woe upon ye,
And all such false professors!
By heaven, my lords, I speak to subjects,
And I'll not tarry here, nor ever more
Upon this business, my appearance make
In any of your courts.

L. C. The Queen is obstinate,
Stubborn to justice, apt to accuse it,

And disdainful to be tried by 't.

She's going away. Call her again.

    Crier. Mary, come into court.

    L. C. Madam, pray you pass not out: I require your
        highness,

That it shall please you to declare, in hearing

Of all these ears, what fault you find with us.

    Q. M. Now the Lord help me! you vex me past my
        patience!

I'm robb'd and bound by subjects. Thieves are not
    judg'd

Except in presence of the judge and their accusers.

Elizabeth is not present, and I

Do beseech your lordships, that in this case of justice,

My accusers (be what they will) may stand

Forth, face to face, and freely urge against me.

    L. C. Nay, that cannot be; we shall give you

The full cause of our coming. If your grace

Could be brought to know our ends are honest,

You'd feel more comfort: why should we, good lady,

Upon what cause, wrong you? Alas! our places,

Our professions, are against it.

    Q. M. My life is innocent from meaning treason

To any royal person, my good lord,

As is the sucking lamb or harmless dove:

But I do know, upon far-fetch'd pretence

Without legal proceeding, this council

Is,—in the interest of your Queen, who is

Asham'd to look upon my hapless death,—sent hither

To work my downfall, and to take away my life.

I cannot weep, for all my body's moisture

Scarce serves to quench my furnace-burning heart;

Nor can my tongue unload my heart's great burden,
For selfsame wind that I should speak withal,
Is kindling coals that fires all my breath,
And burns me up with flames that tears would quench.
Call hither, I say, bid come before me, the false thrall
That hath deluded you: bring forth the gallant:
Let me hear him speak. Ah! what's more dangerous
Than fond affiance in a servant?
Seems he a dove, his feathers are but borrow'd,
For he's dispos'd, as is the hateful raven:
Is he a lamb, his skin is surely lent him,
For he's inclin'd, as is the ravenous wolves,
Who cannot steal a shape that means deceit.
Take heed, my lords, time will bring to light, faults
Now unknown, in the fraudful man, that hath
To save his life, a tale of evil told.

    L. C. O foolish Queen, by this talk, these prattling speeches, you have undone yourself. We are the Queen's subjects and must obey: so, please your highness, the Queen being absent, we entreat you let us begin. My Lord of Lincoln, will you be counsel for her grace? Be pleased to say.

    Lord Lincoln. Nay, my good lord,
For no dislike i' th' world, against the person
Of the good Queen, I may not execute the charge.
With all the rev'rend fathers and learn'd doctors
Of the land in this court, by particular consent,
The daring'st counsel, madam, may be yours.

    Q. M. Even so.
But when I put my sick cause into hands
That hate me, what can hap to me but death?
I have no staff, no stay to lean upon.

Lord Oxford. Stay, gentle Queen,
And hear me speak: vouchsafe to listen what I say,
Perhaps I shall be acceptable to you.

Q. M. My lord,
I do not need your help; if my actions
Were tried by ev'ry tongue, if every eye saw 'em,
Envy and base opinion set against 'em,
I know my life, believe me, could not be
Blotted, but with vile, base and foul abuse.

L. C. Wilt thou accept my Lord of Pembroke?

Lord Pembroke. Your grace,
If my weak oratory can win your highness' safety,
Let me be commanded.

Q. M. My gracious lord,
I will submit my cause to your nobility.

Pemb. May it please you, noble madam, to withdraw
Into your private chamber; I would speak with you.

Q. M. Speak it here;
There's nothing I have done yet, o'my conscience,
Deserves a corner: would all other women
Could speak with as free a soul as I do, my lord.

Lawyer for the Crown. My Lord Chief Justice,
Fie! what an indirect and peevish course
Is this of hers! With a foul traitor's name,
Stuff I her throat! She looks not like a thing
More made of malice than of beauty, though
A parent guilt may well be seen in her.
Oh, that in a Christian climate, souls so refin'd
Should show so heinous, black, obscure a deed as this!
But, thanks be to God,
They accomplish'd not that which they did broach for.
This sweet gentleness did attempt our Sovereign's life,

As is apparent by this letter, writ
In a strange tongue unto the King of France.
In obscure words—full of courtesy, grace
And wit, but empty of matter—she masks her thoughts.
This is unwonted. 'Tis a sign of league
With France, when, with incomparable deep foresight
And dexterity, a mighty monarch
Doth send a messenger to deliver to King Henry such
    a message.
    Q. M. Will you credit
This base drudge's words that speaks he knows not what?
    L. C. Aye, marry will we.
The investigation of this labyrinth,
Doth bring forth two such black monsters, as scarce
Are besmeared in hell.
    Q. M. Take good heed
You charge not, in your spleen, a noble King,
And spoil your soul.
    L. C. Let him on. Go forward.
    Crown Lawyer. On my soul, I'll speak but truth.
I grieve at what I speak, and am right sorry
To repeat what follows: most unwillingly I speak.
Would God that this most noble lady had
Had naught to do, with these numberless offences
'Gainst the English Queen. Beauty's princely majesty is
    such,
That it confounds the tongue and makes the senses rough,
And as the sun plays on the glassy stream,
Twinkling another counterfeited beam,
So seems this gorgeous beauty, to the eyes
Of the weak men who have ta'en oath, to kill
Our royal mistress. She hath a witchcraft

And over them hath cast a spell.
We have found out matter in her letters,
That forever mars the honey of her beauty.
She hath a pretty foot, a cherry lip,
A bonny eye, a passing pleasing tongue,
But she her honey hath steepèd in gall,
And full of great envy and fell jealousy,
To win the crown and usurp the place of our noble Queen,
Hath made suit unto the French King.
The common men she sent, not knowing whom to trust,
Did show her highness' message to the noble Earl
Of Leicester, who spurr'd fast unto our Queen:
Then was this vile treason and outrageous shame,
Which she kindled, unloos'd 'gainst our dread Queen:
The proof of all this cursed plot and traitorous
Design, wherein she hath aspired to deprive
Elizabeth of her crown, betimes hath been
Discovered; the actors have won the meed
Meet for their crimes, and are shut up in prison.
What tongue, my lords, can smooth out, first,
The dissimulation of her grace
And her deep designs against the Queen?
And second, Elizabeth's not being true queen,
The which she doth affirm?   And to conclude,
She must die, or Elizabeth goes down.
     Q. M. Good my lords,
By some putter-on, I am honor-flaw'd!
Command him to come here!   Bring him to the court!
Scarce can I speak, my choler is so great.
Oh, I could hew up rocks and fight with flint,
I am so angry at these abject terms of scorn,
That this saucy merchant, who loves to hear

Himself talk. hath in his dull and long-continu'd speech,
Branded me with. This is excellent sport.¹
Y-faith, that I practiced the Queen's death.
I am not prone to weeping. as our sex
Commonly are, the want of which vain dew.
Perchance, shall dry your pities : but I have
That honorable grief lodg'd here. which I, my lords,
Beseech you all. may so qualify your thoughts
And charities, as shall best instruct you.
Grief and sorrow hath mortified my mind,
Quenching its fire : but let me speak. myself.
Since virtue finds no friends. The cause. I know,
Of all this array, is to rid me of my life ;
It boots not then what I may do. To murder me,
To end my life by subtlety, is the drift
Of this your court ; my accuser is my servant,
And when I did correct him for a fault
The other day, he vow'd upon his knees
He would be even with me. I have good witness
Of this, therefore, let him come into my presence.
The rascal shar'd my bounty, yet he did rob
And pill me : "Let God," said he. "if it please Him,
Care for the many ; I for myself must care
Before all else." And now he would betray me
To my tomb, in hope of gain.

  Burleigh. Doleful dame,
Let not your grief impeach your reverence for truth.
Let her in naught be trusted : the world reports
Ever for speaking false. she hath been noted.

  Q. M. My gracious Lord High Treasurer,
You are a councillor. and by that virtue,
No one dare accuse you. But sir, hear me !

I would you and I knew where a commodity
O' good names were to be bought. When I, in happy
    peace,
Possess'd the crown of Scotland, you were my sworn ser-
    vant,
And made no scruple of taking pieces of gold
From my fingers. You promis'd me to let me pass
Through England unto Paris, and you then betray'd me.
Truly, I dare say without vain glory,
I am far truer spoke than you.

    Bur. My lords,
She'll wrest the sense, and hold us here all day.
Is it well such losers may have leave to speak?

    Q. M. Beshrew the winners, for they play me false!
My heart is drown'd with grief, whose flood begins
To flow within my eyes. Witness my tears,
My body round engirt with misery,
For what's more miserable than ruin of my peace?
False peer, you once did set me up in hope—
For full of prosp'rous hope, by your fair promises,
I into England came. When that rebel Douglas
And his traitorous rout, with a mighty and a fearful head,
Did cast me off, how prettily you play'd
The orator, my lord, and proffer'd peace!
Did I not enter England's ground upon
The offer of your sovereign's love? But you
Shall rue the tears I shed! Upon my death,
My uncle, the French Duke, will become your foe.

    Montague. What if both James and Henry be ap-
    peas'd
By such invention as she can devise?
To have joined with France in such alliance,

Would more have strengthened this commonwealth
Against foreign storms, than any home-bred device.

    Burleigh. Why, know you not, Montague, that of
        itself
England is safe, if true within itself?

    Mont. But th' safer, when 'tis back'd with France.

    Bur. 'Tis better using France, than trusting France:
Let us be back'd with God and with the seas,
Which He hath given for 'fence impregnable,
And with their helps only, defend ourselves;
In them, and in ourselves, our safety lies.
The love I bore you, lo, full again I speak of,
Madam; think you we would let you in France,
An army raise, and as a conqueror return here?
This is no place for Henry's warriors.

    Q. M. Therefore
You played the whole thing! You say nothing, you vil-
        lain!
Hard is the choice, when one is thus compell'd,
Either by silence to die with grief,
Or by speaking, to live with shame.

    Bur. You do me wrong.
I have no spleen against you, nor injustice
For you or any: how far I have proceeded,
Or how far further (shall) is warranted
By my commission. My lords, I will be bold
With time and your attention: mark I pray,
Th' ingratitude of this unworthy woman,
Whose head stands so tickle on her shoulders
That a milkmaid may sigh it off; I will
Acquaint you with the danger to the state:
We may excuse this woman's petty faults

And small offences done, but 'tis impossible
To guard the state, if wayward women shall
Against the realm, reach out rude hands of war.
Sustained by the King of France, and strengthened
By Burgundy and Spain, she hangs o'er our heads,
As did the murd'ring blade o' th' Syracusian King;
The welfare of us all hangs on the cutting short
Of this most cunning traitor.   Proof that she
Hath sought the death of our sovereign,
Thine eyes shall see:
Here is á letter written by herself—
Within, a happy composition, cunningly
Uniting her true policy.   Her suit,
In this device, is to th' deceitful King
Of France, and th' measure of his love is here.
Behold the witness of the aid he promises
Which doth justify her death.
      Q. M. Monster!
Com'st thou with deep, premeditated lines—
With written pamphlets studiously devis'd
Against my life?   If thou canst accuse,
Or aught intend'st to lay unto my charge,
Do it without invention, suddenly,
As I with sudden and extemporal speech
Purpose to answer thee.   Read my letter:
If it could speak, it would inform your worship
Of my regard of your great Queen.
      Bur. Silence,
Thou proud bawd!   Peace, impudent and shameless
      woman!
I have ever wish'd the sleeping of this business,
Never desir'd it to be stirr'd, and have

Hindered oft, the passages made towards it;
But now, I know the secret of thy fraud,
Thy wanton dalliance with a paramour,
The lust o' thy proud cold heart, and how thou hast
By secret means, used intercession
To obtain a league, to take away the life
Of England's royal Queen; I know how thou,
With unlawful oaths, didst get rebellious subjects
To the crown of England, to swear allegiance
To thy majesty; to save our subjects
From massacres and ruthless slaughters, such
As are daily seen in France, we are proceeding
In hostility to thee, and to thy uncle,
The Cardinal of Rome. And let me here
Recount before your grace, how that saucy priest,—
A prelate of the Church,—in a castle keeps
As an outlaw, and useth his spiritual function
To patronage his theft. He hath stept in,
In blood so far, that should he wade no more,
Returning were as tedious as to go o'er:
And thou hast like a baby, ta'en his tenders
Which are not sterling, for true pay; for thee
There's no more sailing by the star of Rome.

    Q. M. Who should be pitiful? Who should study
To prefer peace, if not the consistory of Rome?

      Bur. And yet, these holy churchmen take delight in
        broils;
At their beck, have they not troops of soldiers?
Belike, this good cardinal set on this wretched woman.
Oh, cunning enemy, that t' catch a saint,
With saints doth bait thy hook. Thou, that became
A murtherer for thy lascivious wanton—

Q. M. My lord!
Have you upon these slanders well determin'd?
Are you well warranted with your injuries?
Unless you are, accuse me not of fornication,
Adultery and all uncleanliness.
I slew not my husband.

    Bur. Oh, illegitimate construction!
I warrant thee I will, out of thine own
Confession, show I have not slander'd thee.

    Q. M. Well will you play with reason and discourse,
And can persuade the lords,
Murder and lechery are my conditions.

    Bur. Foul fiend and hag of all despite, encompassed
With thy paramours, didst thou not in thine eye,
Thy hand, thy tongue, bear welcome to beguile
Thy husband to his death?
And didst thou not look like th' innocent flower,
But wast thou not the serpent under it?

    Q. M. Oh, that my nails were anchor'd
In thine eyes! Justice, oh, Justice heaven!
Against this politic sin and wickedness!

    Chief Justice. How now!
What mean you by these outcries in the court,
Where naught should sound but harmonies of speech?

    Q. M. A knavish speech sleeps in a foolish ear, my
        lord:
I want that glib and oily art to speak,
Which is the dowry of this saucy, scurvy fellow,
That hath most wrongfully accusèd me
O' concealèd guilt. Ere I learn to utter English,
This flattering engine of my speech will make void my
        suit.

C. J. What plague afflicts your royal majesty?

Q. M. A prone and speechless dialect my lord:
I would not, else, stand under grievous imposition;
Could I speak fair, what I know is true and false,
I'd bribe you to be an impartial judge.

C. J. How! bribe me? you have marr'd all.

Q. M. Aye, with such gifts
That heaven shall share with you;
Not with fond sickles of the tested gold,
Or stones whose rate are either rich, or poor
As fancy values them: but with true pr٭ yers,
That shall be up at heaven, and enter there
Ere sunrise: prayers from preservèd souls,
From fasting maids, whose minds are dedicate
To nothing temporal.

C. J. Stand aside! This is no time
To jar; you in your frantic mood,
Use speeches which might better have been spar'd.

Q. M. Yet, do you not judge this same time to be
A season to requite the injury
That's offer'd? Heaven shield thee from such woes
As I, thus wronged, receive from this meddler here.

C. J. Stop, your grace; we cannot thus permit
A blasting and a scandalous breath to fall
On him so near us: never yet did he
Misreport your grace.

Q. M. Thieves for their robbery
Have authority, when judges themselves do steal.
Why, all the souls that were, were forfeit once,
And He that might the vantage best have took
Found out the remedy: how would you be,
If He, which is the top of judgment, should

But judge you as you are?　Oh, think on that,
And mercy then will breath within your lips!/

  C. J. Grant that her words bewitch not the commis-
   sion.
'Tis a needful fitness that we
Adjourn this court till further day.

  Q. M. I do perceive these men trifle with me.
My lords of the Council, I will not hence
Till with my talk and tears, both full of truth,
I make him tell, even upon his conscience,
With all dissembling set aside, the truth.
My lord, you must tell why I did desire you
To give me secret harbor.

  C. J. Madam, art thou not asham'd
To wrong him with thy importunacy?

  Q. M. You prove my former speeches: judges give
Judgment according to their own advantage,
Doing to poor innocence manifest wrong.

  C. J. What's this? what's this?
How now!　What means this passion?
Tell me madam, what folly reigns in you?
'Tis a passing shame that you should censure thus,
These lovely gentlemen!　To utter foul speeches
And to detract, will not recover your freedom;
I beseech your majesty not to proclaim us false;
Do no stain to your own gracious person,
Therefore be advised, defaming men
Of good life will not hide your crime;
(If crime it be,) th' dearest o' th' loss is yours.

  Q. M. My lord, the truth you speak doth lack
Some gentleness, and time to speak it in;
You rub the sore when you should bring the plaster.

Indeed, you've spoken truer than you purposèd:
Life I prize not a straw, but I would free mine honor.
You know, my lord, for sixteen years, most villainously
I have been dragg'd about, denied all privilege
Which doth belong to royalty, and lastly,
Have been hurried to this place, and all alone,
Unhappy, am enforc'd to speak for truth:
And I appeal to all the English lords
And barons here, to be unpartial,
As are the gods of destiny; and if
They speak, speak not in my dispraise, but say
"I'm sure she is not false, and did not purpose
To seize on England's Queen;" I crave but this,
For I am as free from touch or soil 'gainst her,
As is the high imperial type of this earth's glory,
With report of it.   For my sake, pity me;
My fainting words do not warrant death.

   C. J. Her words
Enforce these tears, and I shall pity her
If she speaks again.   Away with her!
Madam, I grieve at your declining fall;
Farewell, fair Queen; weep not!   'Tis the Queen's will
That you are subject to this trial; we commit
You to your chamber, until further trial
May be made thereof, if you be guilty.
Come, officer, dismiss the court, I'd fain be gone.
What! are you waking?   Do you not hear me speak?
Break up the court I say.   Set on. [29]   (*Exeunt.*)

---

   29. "And then the court arose and from thence did return
to London, and shortly afterwards the peers met within the
tower these reverend fathers, men of singular integrity and
learning, yea, the elect o' th' land, assembled to plead the
cause of the lovely Queen of Scots.   This in effect was the
Lord Chancellor's speech:—

Scena Secunda.

(*A room in the Tower of London.*)
Lords and Gentlemen Assembled.

Lord Chancellor. Noble peers,
The cause why we are met, is to determine
O' th' falsehood and subtle guile of Scotland.
Ye are the fount that makes the brooks to flow,
And ye are honest men, therefore,
Through your wise speeches and grave conference,
Our sovereign will speak unto the world.
She hath commanded me to say to you,
As you do say shall be, so shall it be;
And in your wisdom she doth trust.
First,—
This woman hath accused the Queen's mother
Of corrupt virtue; you may uprighteously
Do a poor wrong'd lady a merited benefit,
And redeem her name if, peradventure, you
Void not, my lords, this accusation;
Then,—
She hath sent over to the King of France
To discover what power the King hath levied there,
Wherewith to march against the throne of England.
What Christian soldier is there, that will not be
With a religious emulation touch'd,
When he the fierce and manly King of Spain,
Doth see approaching? The heaven's lightning flames
And thunders now, o'er the Low Countries' fatal fields;
And this foul, ambitious woman it is,
Whose wily brain and tongue, with smoothest speech,

Hath tied and tangled him in a dangerous war.
Blood will have blood, and foul murder shall 'scape no
    scourge.
To make away with th' Princess Elizabeth,
(For she doth aspire to the succession)
Is her desire; her inconsistency
And treachery is vain, sith, noble lords,
We've found the proof that her grace did entreat,
With flattering style, St. Peter's chair to talk
Of her title to the English crown,
And did entreat the Pope to aid and succour her.
For those great wrongs, those bitter injuries,
Which she hath offered to England's majesty,
Let Justice put his armour on, and slay her,
Before her chaps be stain'd with crimson blood.
Pray do not stand on quillets how to kill her,
Be it by gynnes, by snares, by subtlety,
Sleeping or waking, 'tis no matter how,
So she be dead, for that is good deceit,
Which mates her first that first intends deceit.

    Burleigh. Thrice noble lord, 'tis resolutely spoke.

    L. C. Not resolute, except so much were done,
For things are often spoke, and seldom meant,
But here my heart accordeth with my tongue.
Then sage, grave men,
Let your counsels sway you in your policy;
Say as you think, and speak it from your souls.

    Montague. My lords,
This be a solemn thing, and should not be
Contemptibly spoken of. Ere she obtain
The crown, to which we humble 'beisance yield,
She first must land here as a conqueror:

And we, in justice, cannot well deny,
That she came not in stealth to hide, but came
In love. I need not cite to you, my masters,
How, when she was a suppliant, that you,—
I speak to you, and you, sir,—you commanded her
To close prison, with many bitter threats
Of biding there. Heaven, it knows, I would
Not have her prove false traitor to our Queen,
But I'll contend, our sovereign's sword will be
Able her sceptre to maintain, without
Touching this poor shadow of a painted Queen.
My noble lords, think not to find me slack
Or pitiful, if she's not fair of faith;
But since your faithful zeal lets me speak, I'm sure
You'll pause awhile, till you are full resolv'd
Of the nature of her defects of grace.
She that you hurt, is of great fame,
And therefore, my gentle lords, history
With full mouth, shall speak freely of our act;
As the matter now stands, if she
Committed fornication in another country,
I must needs say, that though it's not commendable,
Yet it be not odd: even if this is her fault,
Who sinneth most, the tempter or the tempted?
Bethink you!
Who is it that hath died for this offence?
There's many have committed it.

    L. C. Aye, aye, well said.

    Mont. Those who have taken upon them to make
The law of nature a thing of evil, have not been
Effective in quenching and stopping it,
And have done more harm than good. Pray you, look!

We so wipe the justice of our laws away,
That woman now, is an abhorrèd slave;
Where is the antique glory which was wont
In woman to appear? Where be the brave
Achievements done? Where be the battles? Where
The shield and spear? Bin they all dead and laid
In doleful hearse, or do they only sleep,
And shall again awake to force men to put forth
His best advantage? Fair lords, to the plea
Of traitor, there must be verification,
And what I speak, I'll maintain with my sword,
In my mind we have but trivial argument,
More than mistrust, that shows her worthy death.

  L. C. So that, by this, you will not have her die.

  Mont. The sharp and thorny points of my reason
Do drive me forward, and my learnèd lord,
If your grace mark every circumstance, you have
Great reason to do her right, especially
Since, with a flag of truce, she came to us.

  L. C. Betwixt ourselves,
My friends and loving countrymen,
I fear this token serveth for a hollow heart.
See here, Lord Montague, you speak you know not what,
And all too confident. Tut, tut! is she
Too virtuous, mild, or too well given, to dream
Of allegiance with the Pope? Her very cheeks
Would to cinders burn up modesty! I pray
You set to this, yes and the practice of't,—
The letters, to the Kings of Spain and France.
Hath she not deserv'd more than a prison?
Or is there any print of goodness in her?

  Mont. The court must show, this writing of the Queen.

L. C. Enough, sir!
By her writ our Queen hath certified
To us, (which is a matter of record)
This letter, which indeed, we ought to credit:
In our eyes, it may well stand up against
This pretended reason of yours.

    Mont. My lord,
I am sorry for your displeasure, but having
Prerogative of speech thus cast on me,
Come what may come, I will speak stoutly for her.
All will sure be well, for if you only fasten
Your ear to my advisings, I do make
Myself believe, that th' voice and true decision
Of this commission will be rendered
In humanity, and no execution
Done on Mary through suspicion,
Dissimulation, superstition or pride.

    Bur. My lord, right sore aggriev'd am I at this
So sharp reproof, and with most painful feeling
Of your speech, I will learn to begin.
No labor, nor no duty, have I left
Undone. How blind you are! against all sense,
You importune for her: your suit's unprofitable.
We are poisoned by her climbing followers
Who count religion but a childish toy,
And hold there is no sin but ignorance.
I am ashamed to hear such foolery:
She is our enemy, and shall die.
Ha! Doth she not tempt? Lo, saw you that creature
Who for loving this virtuous Queen, to his death hath gone,
You would not intrude her virtue on us.
We have strict statutes and most biting laws,—

The needful bits and curbs to headstrong steeds,—
And I beseech you, let her be condemn'd to die.
Let not this childishness move you; it is
But a soft murmur, and confusèd sound
Of senseless words, which his reason doth impeach,
For guiltiness will speak, though tongues were out of use.
The deeds committed 'gainst the commonwealth
By this red plague, may not be razèd out
Nor longer borne.
She is a murderer; her childhood stain'd,
With blood remov'd but little from her own;
And now doth she stain our great sovereignty,
And hath, in likeness of the adder, stung
(By the very pangs of malice) our wise Queen,
And will, like an eagle in a dove-cote, strike our people.
If thus forewarned, in due prevention
You default, you are not guiltless of crime,
And evermore, all of you deserve blame.
Immediate sentence then, and sequent death,
In reverence of Elizabeth's noble name I beg.
Again I pray you, purge all infection
From our air; let not her cheeks make soft
Your trenchant swords, and spare not her, whose dimpled
    smiles
From fools exhaust their mercy; let not this
Hog in sloth, wolf in greediness, dog in madness,
Lion in prey, plague you with incessant wars.
Do not in obstinacy, cavil at this course;
Ten to one we shall not find like opportunity
Again; therefore, take ye this flattering sin,
Foul as she is and full of sinful blame,
And like true subjects, sons of your progenitors,

Absolve her with the **axe**.

> *L. C.* My lords, what say you?
>
> *All.* Guilty! guilty!
>
> *Kent.* Quick, quick, my lord! I long

To write my name, to urge her punishment
And loudly call for judgment.

> *Bur.* Oh, how joyful am I made by this:
>
> So shall our Queen's wrongs be recompens'd. [30]

(Exeunt.)

Actus Quintus.   Scena Prima.

(*Palace of the Queen.*)

QUEEN ELIZABETH *and her train.*

Queen Elizabeth. Fie! what a slug
Is Warwick, that he comes not to tell us
Whether they will that she shall die or no!
Ah! in good time here comes the sweating lord!

(Enter Warwick.)

Welcome my lord: what will my lords? what is the
        judgment?

> *Warwick.* Your highness, give me leave to breathe;

I have outrun my breath.

---

30. " Thus after many hours of speeches they did set forth
the true way for the expiation and purging of the diseased
soul, that deserved to die. The city of London, on receiving
the report, in the very demonstration and fulness of their cry,
put an end to the false report that they advised the counsel to
spare her, and in their zeal, when they heard she was con-
demned to lose her head, did hail the sentence with such
vehemency, that it was like to madness. The Queen in the
palace staid the coming of the verdict:—

Q. E. Strive man and speak.

War. England hath put a face of gladness on,
Triumphant London doth sing peans loud,
And holy tunes, and sacrifice of thanks
In honor of your name.

Q. E. Think of thy message, sir, and haste thy
tongue.

War. The hideous law, as mice by lions did,
Hath picked out an act, under whose heavy sense,
Her life falls into forfeit:
She's condemn'd, upon the act, to die.

Q. E. It is impossible!

War. Your grace, I tell you true.

Q. E. She is sentenced then to die!
We will proclaim it, and let our subjects see
And know the justice of our court.

War. Your grace, here comes the rest,
Whom, in my haste I left behind.

(*Enter Lords of Council.*)

Q. E. My Lord Chancellor, and Lords,
Thank God, in pity of our hard distress,
And wary in thy studious care, ye have,
In politic council, fixed the Houses
Of Lancaster and York, like a mountain
Not to be removed; our mother's honor ye've redeem'd,
And have again install'd me in the diadem;
Our love and largest bounty we extend to you,
Who are sealed in approbation for thy kind pains.

L. C. Your grace,
Here is the warrant for her death,
Which I tender to your grace, to receive
Your approbation, and may it please you here

To write your princely name.

  Q. E. My lord, I promise
To note it cunningly—but hither come
Th' ambassadors of our brothers of France and Spain.
I know their embassy, and can with ready guess
Declare it, before the Frenchmen speak a word of it.
They crav'd audience, and the hour I think is come
To give them hearing.   Is it four o'clock?

  L. C. It is.

  Q. E. Well then, upon this instant we will hear them.
           (*Enter Ambassadors.*)

Welcome, my noble lords; you're come to us
In happy hour!   Heard you the happy tidings,
How mine honest Council have this day, prov'd their
   virtues,
And after trial, have condemn'd injurious Mary
To the sharpest kind of justice?   Heard you that?

  French Ambassador. Indeed, 'tis true it hath been told
   me.

  Q. E. What think you of it?

  Fr. Am. Alas, I know not what to say.

  Q. E. Answer in the effect of your reputation
And satisfy us, sir.

  Fr. Am. Oh, royal Queen,
In my King's name I am commanded,
By your leave and favor, humbly to kiss your hand;
And if you'll condescend to give me liberty
To speak, I will answer your grace.

  Q. E. Speak what thou wilt.   We did expect thy
   coming.

  Fr. Am. Madam, thus speaks my King:—
Treason is a vice that most I do abhor,

And most desire should meet the blow of justice,
For which I would not plead, but that I must,
For which I must not plead, but that I am
At war 'twixt will, and will not.
Now you are heir to England's throne, therefore enjoy it:
But I do fear, the rigour of the statute
Too close you follow, to make example of her.
Your right depends not on her life or death;
Then seeing this, with reverence be it said,
It resteth in your grace quietly to enjoy your own,
Free from oppression and the stroke of war;
For, if you please, I'll undertake your grace
Shall well and quietly enjoy your realm,
Upon condition I may ransom her; and so
Shall you be happy, free, as England's royal Queen.

    Q. E. That is, if we deliver her up to Henry?
We give thee kingly thanks!
To be a queen in bondage, is more vile
Than is a slave in base humility.
Dost thou not know the army of this Queen
Means to besiege us?   Dost thou not know
That naught but gall, venom and wicked words,
That God and men offend, is in her lying tongue,
Which in two parts divided is, and both the parts do speak?
And as her tongue, so is her heart,
That never thought one thing but doubly.
Therefore, the bloody knife shall play the umpeere,
Arbitrating 'twixt our extremes and us!

                        (*Enter Messenger.*)

But stay! what news?   Why comest thou in such post?
    Mess. It is rumor'd the King of Spain's great navy
Doth land at Milford Haven.

Q. E. How say you, my lord Ambassadors?
We turn to thee, my Lord of Spain;
Let us hear your grant or your denial.

Spanish Ambassador. Madam,
It is not true; if it were true, the salve
For such a sore would be but to be wise,
And shut such neighbors out of door.

Q. E. We see thy wit,
But answer straight, and not with foolish boldness.

Sp. Am. In regard, then, of the great force that
    rumour
Doth land upon your kingdom,—rumour is
Full of surmises, jealousies, conjectures,
And when commenced on this ball of earth,
Doth grow like hydra's head,—on my honor, gentle lady,
King Philip, my master, hath not set forth
War for Britain, for had he left my native country
T' depose your grace, if I should stand before you,
To cry you mercy for the meanest of your land,
I should be forsworn. I' God's name, turn me away,
And let the foul'st contempt shut door upon me,
If you believe our trumpets clamorous speak,
Harbingers of blood and death, within your realm.
Pardon my answer, madam, if it appear not civil,
But if you've any justice, any pity,
If you be anything but a tyrant,
Pluck not away the life of a lady
Of the blood of France.

Q. E. It is the law, not I, condemns her.

Sp. Am. Yet show some pity, madam.

Q. E. I show it most of all when I show justice:
For then I pity those I do not know,

Which a dismiss'd offence would after gaule.
Many had not dared to do evil,
If the first that did the edict infringe
Had answer'd for his deed. Now the angry law's awake,
Takes note of what is done, and like the prophet
Looks in a glass that shows what future evils,
Either now, or by remissness, new conceiv'd,
And so in progress to be hatch'd, and born,
Are now to have no successive degrees,
But here they live to end.

  Fr. Am. If she be guilty, as 'tis published,
Nor prince nor peer may deny your grace's right,
However sinister the doom,
To send her unto judgment; but who are they
That accuse her of fornication?
Wretches who are no more but instruments
Of some more mighty member that sets them on.
Let me have way, your grace, to find this practice out.

  Q. E. Aye, with my heart,
And punish them to your height of pleasure.

  Fr. Am. Madam, may I then write unto my king
That your highness will pardon her?

  Q. E. My lord,
She hath confessed to the vile encounters
They have a thousand times, in secret had.
They are not to be named, my lord—not to
Be spoken of—there is not chastity enough
In language, without offence to utter them.

  Fr. Am. I know not how to pray your patience,
Yet I must speak : choose your revenge yourself;
Impose on me what penance your invention
Can lay upon my sin, but by my soul,

I'm forced to speak for her.

    Q. E. Aye, but we fear
You speak upon the rack, where men, enforc'd,
Speak anything.

    Fr. Am. I should be guiltier
Than my guiltiness, to think I can be
Undiscernable! I perceive your grace, like power divine,
Hath look'd upon my secret counsel. My King
Hath show'd himself sensible and almost
Prescient of this event, and he hath, with full line
Of his authority, imposed upon me
Absolute power.

    Q. E. We must confess, we have heard so much,
And thought to have spoke thereof, but being overfull
Of self affairs, our mind did lose 't. But come,
You speak as having power! Look you that you
Do arm yourself to fit your fancies to our will,
Or else the law of England yields you up,
Which by no means we may extenuate,
To death. Be well instructed, and prepar'd
How to carry yourself in this your embassage:
Keep to a moderate carriage and bearing,
Or we will undertake to make you. We will take
You hence to th' rack and towze you joint by joint!

    Fr. Am. Madam, you are unjust; you dare no more
Stretch this finger of mine, than you dare rack your own!
I'm not your subject nor provincial here.

    Q. E. Do you tax us with injustice? Do you so, sir?

    Fr. Am. Madam, you have bereft me of all words ·
Only my blood speaks to you in my veins,
And there is much confusion in my powers.

    Q. E. Hark, sir! Would you

Close now, after you accuse us
Of injustice? Oh, this false woman misus'd us
Past the endurance of a block! an oak
With but one green leaf on it would have answer'd her;
And now you wonder much that we should put
This shame and trouble from us. Set her free?
If now 'twere fit to do't,—after th' imperious
Language of your King,—by Holy God, we would not
        free her!
No, faith, not if he and all his lords came here
To succour her. Goodness is never fearful!
We have a spirit to do anything
That appears not foul, and in the truth of our spirit,
Virtue is bold. She's worthy of death—fire cannot melt
That opinion out of us—and you waste all
In making question of her innocence!
'Tis almost five o'clock, and so, farewell.
Yet ere you go, my lords of France and Spain,
We have some private schooling for you both;
You cannot climb o'er the house to unlock the gate,
Therefore, to study now to free her is too late. [31]

                                                    (*Exeunt.*)

---

31. "Thus my mother broke up the audience, and stayed
not for an answer. And yet, nor scroll nor parchment, bears
the Queen's warrant for the death of Princess Mary, though
she was beheaded."

"You are pleasant, sir, and speak apace. Why, what a
truthless thing is this! How was the warrant obtained?"

"By treachery. Lo, sir, here's the three crafty men that
bewrayed the fair lady."

"Who are they, sir?"

"The most redoubted peers in England: William Cecil,
Lord High Treasurer, my father, the Earl of Leicester, and
M. Secretary of the Queen. Stand thou aloof and hear how
the matter grows:—

Scena Secunda.

(*Street in London*)

Enter my LORD OF BURLEIGH *and Secretary of the Queen* on one side and my LORD OF LEICESTER *on the other.*

Lord Burleigh. Fairly met, my old and faithful friend,
I am glad to see you, my good earl.
Lord Leicester. Many
And hearty thankings to you both.
Bur. My lord, I crave you
Lend me your knees, and all my life to come,
I'll lend you all my life to do you service.
L. L. Faith, my lord, go to your knees and make
ready.
Bur. I spoke it but according to the trick ;
Would't please you that the Princess Mary perish ?
L. L. Oh, my good lord,
They say best men are moulded
Out o' faults, and for the most, become much more
The better for being a little bad ;
I think she's so out of love with life
That she will sue but to be rid of it.
But, my lord, I have no superfluous leisure ;
My stay must be stolen out of other affairs.
Farewell.
Bur. Hold ! Might you dispense with your leisure,
I'd have some speech with you.
L. L. I will attend you.
Bur. Very good, let us in this house here.

(*Enter a Constable.*)

Ha ! constable,
What house is this ?

Constable. It be a bawd's house, sir.
It is a naughty house.   She be a woman
Cardinally given that lives here, sir.

 Bur. Hold here!   Inquire of her if gentlemen
Can lodging have to speak privately.

(Exit Constable.)

My good lord, will you sit it out here, or go home?
If this occasion was not virtuous
I should not urge it half so faithfully.

 L. L. I've sworn to stay with you, my lord.

 Bur. Behold where Madam Mitigation comes.

(Enter Bawd.)

 Bawd. And 't please you, my lords, enter.

Scena Tertia.

(*Room in* BAWD'S *House.*)
LORDS BURLEIGH, LEICESTER *and* SECRETARY DAVISON.

 Burleigh. My lord,
For her death I had a written warrant once,
But by great misfortune, late it lost; and this
To remedy, I have bid Davison,
Who has a valiant mind,—which makes me love,
Admire and honor him,—to write another.
How say you?

 Lord Leicester. I say, wisdom wishes to appear
Most bright, when it doth tax itself,
As black masks proclaim an enshield beauty
Ten times louder than beauty could display'd;

But I will speak more gross, and I know this
To be true; our dear lady, within this hour, said :—
"Oh woe is me, all too long this peril
To the state doth 'scape the scourge that waits on death.
I wonder it should be thus!   I burn to hear
That she is dead! then will I be content."

   Secretary. Why do you put these sayings upon me?

   L. L. Because you are secretary—there's the plain
    truth—
And can, if it shall pleasure you, cure the disease
And remove the chief cause that concerns her grace.

   Sec. Believe me, I'm not glad that this is so ;
I dare not, my lord, serve you in this.

   Bur. What! canst thou object?

   Sec. I do beseech your grace to pardon me :
I am earnest in your service, but, my good lord,
Honor and policy like unsevered friends
I' th' wars, do grow together.

   L. L. Grant that, yet
For your best ends, will you adopt this policy ;
Because it now lies on you to displant this woman
Who doth rear high her head, like a luxuriant plant
That comes of the lust of the earth without
Any formal seed, against her majesty.

   Sec. My lord, you push me hard ; I say I dare not.
Have you no poison mixed, no sharp ground-knife,
No sudden mean of death ?

   L. L. How sir!   Think'st thou
I am an executioner?   There is a kind
Of character in thy life, that to th' observer
Thy history fully unfolds ; thyself
And thy belongings are not thine own ; thy virtues

Are rubbish. Now I'll speak to be understood.

Sec. Speak on.

Bur. Forbear sharp speeches, my lord.

L. L. This matchless virtue angers me; let him
Give ear to our request, and show devotion
And a right Christian zeal, to his sovereign
And th' business of the state, and in addition,
So earn our love, and not our deadly spite.

Sec. My lord,
What is your gracious pleasure? Dare you speak it?

Bur. That you sign this warrant, which is
The order for her overthrow.

Sec. Why then,
Your grace would make me write the Queen's name!
I shall suffer death!—for certain I will!

L. L. Stay, fear not!
We, of evil deeds, must choose the least,
And to save her grace, for I tender the safety
Of my Queen, it is our duty to rid her of her foes;
It is no murder in a Queen, to end
Another's life to save her own.

Sec. Aye, lords,
Thou art i' th' right, and I will do't although
I lose my life.

Bur. I thank you! But why lose we time?
Here is the warrant, and I pray you, sign
Her royal name unto it. Hoa, there! fetch me
Pen and ink.   (*Enter maid with pen, ink and paper.*)
So, set it down and leave us.

                                   (*Exit maid.*)

Write here. But I do bend my speech to one
That can teach me.   (*Secretary signs the Queen's name.*)

Sec. There, please your honors, I think
If you are not critical, that will do.

Bur. I am sure it will. Here is my hand. The deed
Is worthy doing.

L. L. And so say I.

Sec. And I.

Bur: And now we three have spoke it,
It skills not greatly who impugns our doom.
But now, sir, away, away!

(Exit Secretary.)

Come my lord,
Wend we to th' court; I'll tell thee more of this
Another time as I need not fish more
With this bait, for this fool gudgin;
You were bold in your foolery.

L. L. Oh! he is but an asse unpolicied. [32]

(Exeunt.)

---

32. "Now, my lord, repair with me to the castle where
dwelleth the fair lady; for my lords with their trains are now
in progress, and if we delay, we shall not see her die."

"I obey you, sir. When must she die?"

"As I do think, tomorrow."

"Then all the help of Scotland should be bent to rescue
her."

"True, but they know not of the intent. But, my lord,
here is her prison; let us unto her chamber:"—

▲

Scena Quarta.

(*Chamber in Fotheringay Castle.*)
QUEEN MARY *and Maids. Enter a Gentleman.*

Queen Mary. How now?

Gentleman. And't please your grace, the English Lords
Wait in the presence.

Q. M. Would they speak with me?

Gent. They willed me to say so, madam.

Q. M. Pray their graces
To come near. What can be their business
With me a poor weak woman, fallen from favor?
I do not like their coming, now I think on't.

(Enter English Lords.)

Welcome, my lords; why do you come? is't for my life?

Lord Shrewsbury. 'Tis now dead midnight and by
eight tomorrow,
Thou must be made immortal.

Q. M. How, my lord!
Tomorrow? tomorrow? Oh, that's sudden!
Oh, this subdues me quite! Oh, fie upon thee,
Slanderer, I know it is not true!

Lord Kent. It is true,
Or else I am a Turk; therefore, prepare
Yourself for death; do not your resolution
Satisfy with hopes that are fallible;
Tomorrow you must die.

Q. M. Why then, thou art
An executioner! and so I am to die.

Well, if I must die, I will encounter darkness
As doth a bride, and hug it in my arms.
Good friend, I remember thee by th' sound o' thy voice;
I met thee at the trial; I would fain
Have come to me some holy friar.

    Kent. Dame,
Not e'en for all this land would I be guilty
Of so great a sin.   God forbid we should
Infringe upon the holy privilege
Of blessed God.

    Q. M. Sir, even for our kitchens,
We kill the fowl of season; shall we serve heaven,
With less respect than we do minister
To our gross selves?   Good, good my lord, if I
Must die tomorrow, let me have some reverend
Person t' advise, comfort and pray with me.

    Kent. Ere we can take due orders for a priest,
You will be dead.   I would desire you, madam,
To clap into your prayers, straightway, for, look you,
The warrant's come.

    Q. M. I will have more time to prepare me—
I am not fitted for death.   O sir, spare me,
I beseech you! spare me! spare me, ye English peers,
Until my ghostly shriver give me shrift!

    Kent. Be silent!
I'll teach you how you shall arraign your conscience,
And try your penitence, if it be sound,
Or hollowly put on.

    Q. M. I'll gladly learn.

    Kent. Look you, get you a prayer-book in your hand,
And stand between two churchmen of our profession,
And then for mercy kneel at the feet of God.

Q. M. Have done, my lord.
The Church of Rome forefend
That I should be author to dishonor it!
But where is thy warrant to approach my presence?

  Kent. Look thou, here is the hand and seal o' th'
    Queen;
I doubt not thou knowest the character,
And th' signet is not strange; until that thou
Canst rail the seal from off this warrant,
Thou but offend'st thy lungs to speak so loud.

  Q. M. Slander
To thy dismal seal! We give to thee our guiltless blood,
Thou unreverend and unhallowed hound!
Of many heinous crimes thou stand'st condemn'd;
May heaven lay on thee my curse!

  Kent. Unhallowed or holy,
The Queen, and Parliament, hath physic for your rank-
    ness!
I stand for law.

  Q. M. And for standing by, let the devil
Be honor'd for his burning throne! away!
Call my gentlewomen! hardly shall we have time,
To wrap our bodies in black mourning gowns
And number our Ave-Maries with our beads,
And our devotions tell, before the hour
Shall be here when my head must fall; therefore,
Get you gone, my lords, and leave me 'mong my maids.[33]
            (*Exeunt.*)

---

33. " Come, my lord, let's quit this chamber and see the
ingenious way these torturers did use to express the same.
Here is the room, which for forty days hath been hung in

Scena Quinta.

(Hall of Fotheringay Castle, hung with black. Platform and block at one end.)
English peers, Executioner and Assistant.
Enter QUEEN MARY, *dressed in a black and red velvet gown.*

Executioner. Pray, mistress, pardon me! I never
    have cut off
A woman's head; but thou wilt feel no pain.
    Queen Mary. Oh, God forgive my sins, and pardon
    thee!
I offer thee, hoodwinked as thou art,
My hand to kiss, because thou art not void of pity:

black, with nothing in it but the platform and the block.
Not content with this, they very oft have waked her, as if to
carry her to execution, and showed her a seeming warrant."

"I will lay myself in hazard that she, whom here they
have a warrant to execute, is no greater forfeit to the law than
she who hath sentenced her. Methinks her execution is nothing less than bloody tyranny."

"Silence, speaking the truth is dangerous in this fair age."

"By heaven, I cannot flatter, I defy the tongue of sooth-
ers, but a braver place in my heart's love hath no man than
yourself. Nay task me to my word. Approve me, lord."

"Thou hast redeemed my lofty opinion of thee, and
showed thou makest some tender of my life in this speech.
But the Queen is here at hand, and you must not speak; stand
you awhile aloof. Yet see, sweet lord, how royally, and yet
with what simpleness she is arrayed. See her red-black, three-
piled, velvet gown, wraught with great care, that like covered
fire, doth make the rare beauty of her face appear, which is
as a book, where men may read strange matters practiced. O
never more shall sun see that fair face! For through high
heaven's grace, which favours not the wicked gifts 'gainst
loyal princes, she with shadows of vain hope inspired, is here
brought to her sad doom. Lo, where comes her train, and the
common executioner:"—

And I desire thee make thou quick dispatch;
And do not wrong me as a slaughterer doth,
Who giveth many wounds when one will kill.

    Ex. Upon my faith and troth, believe me,
I'll be as sure and speedy in your end,
As all the poisonous potions in the world.

    Q. M. My lords, I pray ye attend! Ye charge me that
        I have
Blown a coal of war, between France, Spain and England:
And that I laid a trap as well,
To take your Queen's life; I do deny it:
I never dream'd upon this damnèd deed:
Remember how under oppression I do reck,—
Shut up; forbid to speak the ceremonial rites
Of Rome; no priest, no prelate, no holy father
To tell of peace to my sick soul, attends me;
No prayers nor masses to resolve my sins,
And to give ease unto my smart and wounds,—
It is not to be endur'd! and if you tell
The heavy story right, upon my soul,
The hearers will shed tears; yea, even my foes
Will shed fast falling tears, and say it was
A piteous deed to take me from the world,
And send my soul to heaven! My blood upon your
        heads!
And in your need, such comfort come to you,
As now I reap at your too cruel hands.
I pray you will present to th' Queen of England,
A handkerchief steep'd in my blood; and say to her,
That it did drain the purple sap from my sweet body,
And bid her wipe her weeping eyes withal.

    Kent. Have done, have done; this cannot save you.

Q. M. I blush to see a nobleman want manners.

Kent. I had rather want those than want my head.

Q. M. Good my lord, I pray you, speak not;
What mischief and what murder, too, alas
Hath been enacted through your enmity.

(*She kneels and prays.*)

Oh God, have mercy upon me, and receive my fainting
soul again. Oh, be thou merciful! And let our princely
sister be satisfied with our true blood, which, as thou
knowest, unjustly must be spilled! O God, send to me
the water from the well of life, and, by my death, stop
effusion of Christian blood, and 'stablish quietness on
every side! Let me be blessèd for the peace I make.
Amen.

(*Rises.*)

Lords, I have done, and so I take my leave:
And thus I seal my truth, and bid adieu,
Sweet Shrewsbury and my loving Montague, to you.
And all, at once, once more farewell, farewell.
Sweet lords, let's meet in heaven.
Good my lord of Derby, lead me to the block.

(*To the Executioner.*)

Sirrah, take good heart; cheer thy spirits,
And strike my head off with a downright blow:
Come, mortal wretch, be angry and dispatch.

(*Exeunt Omnes.*)

www.ingramcontent.com/pod-product-compliance
Lightning Source LLC
Chambersburg PA
CBHW020255090426

42735CB00009B/1093